Writing Is Our Superpower

A Mental Health Anthology

Various AATA Authors

Introduction by Sarah Michelle Lynch

I'VE ALWAYS LOVED LIFE. IN that way I am incredibly privileged. Annoyingly, I revel in the changing of the seasons, I find beauty in dead things and darkness. I see pain in people even when they're smiling; and in that, too I see beauty; that thing we call humanity, so fragile, raw and painful. I enjoy simple things like reading, taking a walk, watching strangers laugh or argue. The smell of the sea, dirt in my nails, backache from a hard day's labour, blistered feet after a good night out. Where most people see annoyance, I see privilege. I see life and that thing Shakespeare wrote about: "So long as men can breathe, or eyes can see, So long lives this, and gives life to thee." Every day I chase that new chance to *be* and to *do* and to *explore*.

From when I was young, I sought experiences, searched for connections, and those have sustained and nourished me, and have remained a steadying influence to this day. I still want to know more about people and their lives. Which is why I'm organising the "Authors at the Armouries" book signing event... and this book of essays on mental health. I love to be educated, to know about "taboo" issues and all the unique experiences people go through. I want to know about things I'm not familiar with. I want to understand and be enlightened.

The closest I ever came to a mental health blip was last year. I remember telling someone I was feeling flatline and kind of blah. I honestly think it was a combination of this thing we've all suffered through – covid fatigue – mixed with a death in the family, my husband having a career crisis and everyone else around me generally falling apart. I'm usually the person people turn to. I'm the one people remark on with the words, "We don't need to worry about Sarah."

It can be hard when people have that impression of you, as though you are impervious. Especially when you work so hard and a lot of the time that is taken for granted. Yet it's true that I am stronger than most. I've had to be. The danger is these roles we get pigeonholed into can stick and every single one of us needs room for manoeuvre sometimes. None of us knows what lies around the corner and putting people into boxes is rather last century, when you think about it. (Or it should be.) We're changing all the time, every single one of us, and sometimes you can go from being the "strong" one to suddenly needing to enforce boundaries so you can regroup. And that's okay.

My life hasn't been perfect but on numerous occasions, I've been lucky enough to be able to say that cliché thing: "This too shall pass" which it does for most people. Time marches on, you look back and that terrible time you went through seems long ago, far away and a blip. Many of us don't realise quite how happy we were until we're not; such is the way of life; lessons are sprung on us all the time, out of nowhere.

The leading cause of death among men under 50 is suicide (in the UK at least). It tells me we still have a long way to go surrounding men's mental health and in offering safe spaces for men to feel okay to talk. It is alarming and saddening to say the least. Young people are also at a greater risk than ever before and there have been calls for more education in schools.

Indeed, I had a friend when I was younger who had mental health struggles and sometimes it was impossible to try and help her. I always felt like there was this enormous barrier to truly knowing her even though she was a funny, warm and bright person. There was a chasm nobody could bridge – not even me, a highly attuned empath. She was one of those people who'd give every encouragement to others and none to herself.

It was really difficult to understand why she was the way she was and a lot of our other friends would dismiss her and use her as fodder for gossip, the butt of a joke. She died young of complications during a hospital stay and I truly believe if she'd had better mental health, perhaps she might be alive today. But maybe that's just me still trying to cope with it, all these years later. When someone was such a big part of your formative years, it's almost unbelievable when they're gone.

She was there when I first met my husband and gave me this mini lecture about hanging onto this one. I still remember her words "you will make it, you're both strong" as if she could see it all stretching out ahead of us. Or maybe she thought from her point of view that it takes enormous courage to let your guard down with another person. I never saw that at the time. I was just a wild young woman in love. I didn't know then that along the way, I would discover so much about myself as I leaned in to someone else. That I would change and become a different person entirely as I negated my selfish self to help and grow with another. I didn't see then that we would have to weather storms beyond our imagination.

Through it all, I've found, it is the few and treasured, genuine, selfless, true connections, bonds and relationships we cultivate that get us through – that make the difference.

But as we know, sometimes, there are just some problems that can't be solved with a listening ear or medication, nor a holiday or a change of career. What about the things we can do nothing about?

Those times when it all feels... hopeless.

Situations we just have to come to terms with, hour by hour, day by day.

Maybe just to know you're not alone helps?

Solutions you might not have known about... perhaps you might find a place to start right here, between these pages.

The struggles, frustrations, sorrows and heartening experiences you're about to read offer a plethora of perspectives. This thing we call mental health is complex and an ever-evolving discussion.

I'm so thankful to everyone who's contributed and I pray we can help many people with this book. If we evoke the odd smile, or a cathartic tear or two... we did our job.

Most importantly, I hope, these essays start some very important conversations.

For some sufferers it can feel like you might choke on the words before you've even uttered them. It can be just too hard to say what's really going on.

You see, that's where the written word comes in.

It's truly a superpower.

Put pen to paper and even if you never share those words with another soul, it's a start and can often mark the beginning of acceptance, healing and the build up to those three words most of us find loath to utter: *I need help*.

You are never, ever alone. Here is the proof...

Love, Sarah x

LIVING WITH BIPOLAR
by Anne Wedgwood

WHAT DO YOU KNOW ABOUT bipolar disorder? For most people, it's probably nothing more than a mention in the news when a celebrity in crisis tells us they've been coping with it for years. Or perhaps from watching a TV programme telling you how they've managed it. It's good to know that it's not taboo to talk about it in the way that it might have been in the past, but when bipolar enters your life, nothing can prepare you for what lies ahead for the simple reason that every case is as different as the people who have been diagnosed.

My husband, Bruce, was diagnosed with Bipolar I in 2004, after two depressions in his twenties, a psychotic episode and sectioning in 2002, fifteen years of marriage and three children. The earlier depressions were bad, but apparently circumstantial and ultimately resolved, and the sectioning in 2002 was viewed as a potentially isolated event. By the time the episode of 2004 occurred, life appeared to be back to normal, and we knew nothing about bipolar or what it meant when the diagnosis was made. Perhaps there's more information available now, but Bruce was pretty much sent home from the hospital with instructions to 'keep taking the tablets' and not much more. Subsequent years saw episodes and hospitalisations every few years until a wonderful consultant recognised that the meds weren't right, changed them, and opened the door to a period of wellness which has lasted nearly six years.

The first episode followed a long period of what you might call a 'minor high', with Bruce taking on more and more activities, and gradually becoming obsessed with his Christian faith. Later ones happened more quickly, sometimes escalating in a matter of days, but always centred on religion. We don't attend church any more as it could all too easily lead to another episode, and the most recent one took the form of a psychotic depression with psychosomatic physical symptoms, taking us both by surprise, as these hadn't occurred previously. Bruce's symptoms have always escalated rapidly, with very limited opportunities to address the situation before an episode requiring hospitalisation ensues. It's easy to say 'look for the signs', and now that Bruce is stable, we are much better at identifying and responding to these at a relatively low level, but it's taken a long time. Earlier and more serious episodes can be related to meds not working or stressful periods in our lives. Early signs are easy to see in retrospect, but this is a complex and challenging condition, and the signs and symptoms won't always be the same, even for the same person.

If you've been diagnosed or live with someone who has been, there are certainly challenges ahead, but there are strategies and resources which have helped us both over the years, and which could, I hope, be of help to others. The most important thing is to remember that everyone is different – a strategy that works for one person won't necessarily be right for you. Having said that, here is our story, which could give you a few ideas.

There's no short answer as to how to cope with bipolar, but an understanding of the condition is a start. The internet was in its earlier stages in 2004, but even if it hadn't been, I think we'd have been too much in shock and coping with the fallout of an episode and hospitalisation to really take much in. I suppose the converse problem is now the case, with too much information available to take in all at once. So my advice would be to find out the bare bones and stop there. There are so many stories of people's experiences out there, but ultimately very few will be relevant to you, because – sorry for the repetition – everyone is different. Bruce and I have read, watched and heard about a lot of bipolar people's experiences, and most of them are a world away from what we have experienced ourselves. It's good to know you're not alone, but be wary of expecting other people's experiences to give you an easy answer.

Top tip number two – it sounds obvious, but if you are given medication, take it! There's often an assumption that it's good when you 'come off' medication. This might be the case for a contextual condition such as depression, but bipolar's not like that. You wouldn't expect to be able to stop taking medication for a heart condition, would you? Bipolar is no different – it's not going to go away. It's hard to get the meds right – the condition can worsen, the body can build up resistance, and everyone is different. I'm sure some people are given the meds that are 'right' for them immediately, but I think it is far more common to need to tinker with them over time to find what works best for you. We have come across a common – and understandable – view amongst health professionals that as long as your meds keep you out of hospital, they are working. It took us a long time to recognise that this isn't enough. If you're not feeling right – perhaps depressed or unreasonably tired – say so, and ask for a review. Changing meds is a complex and sometimes scary business, and it needs support, but it will be worth it in the end.

This relates to a common challenge – getting the help you need. Having moved from 'down South' to Yorkshire in 2007, we found a definite – and positive - difference in care, and it can't be denied that access to mental health care is a national problem. Sadly, it seems that help is often only available when a patient is in crisis, and not always then. Bruce has a great talent for appearing to be fine when he isn't, and there have been times at both ends of the country when I have needed to act extremely assertively in order to ensure his admittance to hospital. Don't be afraid to argue your point. You know your situation best, and others may need you to explain what can't be readily seen. On one occasion I told an A & E nurse that I would leave the house locked up so that Bruce wouldn't be able to get back in and told her to ask him to give her his bible – this was a major trigger for him, and she quickly changed her mind! Another time, I said I would hold the NHS responsible for any damage done to the house or to himself if Bruce wasn't admitted, getting him to sign a document agreeing with me – this also did the trick.

As I said before, bipolar can be managed, but it doesn't go away – there isn't a 'cure'. It can be a real challenge to explain this to family and friends, particularly those who you don't see regularly. If things are going well, the bipolar person can seem to be fine to others, particularly in social contexts, and you may find yourself struggling day to day only to find other people failing to understand what you are having to cope with. It is likely to take time to find out who is going to be able to listen and understand the situation once you have moved on from the crisis point of diagnosis to the longer-term context of living with the condition. Try not to get cross at people for underestimating the severity of the condition – it's hard for anyone to understand anything they're not living with on a day-to-day basis. Try to accept people's different levels of understanding – even when they tell you that they're 'a bit bipolar' themselves!

Top tip number three is to establish a routine. Bruce was offered some cognitive behaviour therapy (CBT) sessions shortly after coming to Yorkshire. These enabled him to identify some very helpful routines which I believe have helped him to avoid falling into depression. He began to structure his day around activities which he enjoyed and which supported his well-being, such as walking, reading and playing the piano, combined with collecting children from school and household chores. Setting up a productive routine removed the need to make decisions every day and ensured he didn't lie in bed all day. Having a dog also helped, as it was Bruce's job to walk her while I was out at work, giving him no excuse to miss taking the exercise which is so beneficial to mental health. The children are grown up now and the dog died a few years ago, but the routines are still in place after more than a decade. If any of the elements of reading, music or exercise are missing for more than a day or two, we notice an immediate effect on his mood, reminding us of how crucial these activities are to Bruce's well-being.

The impact of CBT can be enormous, but only if it comes at the right time and with the right focus. Although the routines helped Bruce to stay well, his meds at the time left him listless and disengaged, and it wasn't until sometime later that this changed, after the effects of the meds had led him to stop taking them. Although it's vital to take your meds, we have learnt that if you want to stop, this is a sign that they're not working. It has happened to Bruce twice and the second time resulted in a full review and transfer to new ones whilst he was in hospital. When he came home, he was able to access further CBT which helped him to explore his condition, including the many highs and lows he had experienced over the years. This helped him to identify the times when the periods of what he terms 'exuberance' which are part of his condition had led to good things happening. He regularly refers to the visual timeline which he constructed as part of this process, and this positive reinforcement of the good things in his life is an important part of his continued wellness.

It's hard to access CBT, particularly if you've not recently been in crisis, but these strategies of routine and reflection might be helpful nonetheless. And it's important to remember that CBT isn't a magic bullet. It needs to be the right help at the right time to be effective, and it's up to you what you do with it afterwards. There's no point in learning how important routines are if you don't stick to them in the long term. And looking back over your life will be far more meaningful and supportive if you do it regularly rather than as a one-off event.

On leaving hospital, Bruce has been assigned community psychiatric nurses (CPNs) to support him in those first few weeks and months. If you are fortunate enough to be able to access this resource, use it, but make sure that it is in a way that works for you. Health professionals will have lots of ideas as to how they can help you or what you can do to aid recovery, but they won't all be right for you, and you shouldn't be afraid to say so. Some people will benefit from doing voluntary work or joining a walking group, but for others it will be a nightmare. Start from your 'normal' point – if you hated cooking before you became unwell, it's unlikely that learning to bake will help you now. I eventually had to explain this to a very well-meaning CPN, along with the suggestion that Bruce should focus on doing what he enjoyed most before his episode.

It's a similar thing with support groups. It can be enormously helpful to engage with online forums, and there are plenty out there to choose from. I'm sceptical as to their use for a bipolar person, simply because everyone's condition and experiences are so different, but I am sure there are plenty of people out there who have found them helpful. Just be careful not to expect too much of yourself if you read comments from people who are in a period of relative wellness. It can be very dispiriting to read about people working in high-powered jobs while you are struggling to get out of bed in the morning. This can be particularly problematic when people with Bipolar I and II are communicating in the same forum. This is not the place to go into the differences between the two conditions, but they are significant enough to present a potential challenge in shared groups.

I engaged in an online group for partners of bipolar people for about a year, a few years after Bruce's diagnosis. I found it helpful at first but left after a few months, partly because I didn't have time to cope with all the emails landing in my inbox, but also because of the extreme variance of experiences. It led me to look for more specific support, which I found through Rethink. I didn't want to engage in group discussions, but they were able to put me in touch with another person supporting a bipolar husband in similar circumstances. We provided a listening ear for each other over a period of about a year, which was very helpful at the time. There's no 'best' support, but there may be times when talking to others in the same position as you will be helpful, whether it is you or your partner who is bipolar. The important thing is to work out what you need and find the best way to get it. Remember that this may change over time, and if it starts to make you feel worse, not better – stop!

The most important advice I would give to anyone with bipolar is to treat it as a job. You'll need to keep doing this for the rest of your life, and the better you get at it, the better your life will be. Some of this involves practical stuff like taking your meds and maintaining positive routines. But things change, and you'll be better off if you prepare for them. Every bipolar person will have signs that something is not right. Even when you're in a period of wellness there can be days when you're not so great. Bruce has regular 'blips' where his thoughts will start racing off in unhealthy directions. We have both learnt to recognise these and to develop strategies to stop them escalating. Looking at his timeline and remembering the positive outcomes of his condition helps, and he has his 'little book'. This is where he has written advice for himself in the form of a few simple statements about how he feels when he is well, to help him calm down if he gets agitated.

Reducing stress has been a huge part of maintaining Bruce's wellness, and we have developed strategies to help with this that are now part of our daily lives. Bruce suffers from anxiety, so I never leave the house without telling him when I'll be back – and I call if I'm going to be late. I have to work away from home for a few nights each month, and I always write down the times I will be calling him each evening – and stick to it! Holidays or visits to friends are planned so as to remove any possibility of stress, and we plan our social lives very carefully, as Bruce finds too much interaction with others very tiring. He doesn't have a phone or use the internet at all, and we both believe this is hugely important in maintaining his equilibrium. I know some people look at us and think I do more than my share of tasks around the house, and I do, so that Bruce can stay well. He is battling every day to stay on an even keel to make sure he stays well. Keeping life simple and reducing stressful situations in this way supports this and allows us to enjoy life together.

If you're the partner or carer of a bipolar person, be sure to look after yourself too. There may be times when you need to 'do your own thing' simply in order to maintain your capacity to be supportive. Meeting friends and maintaining hobbies can be a huge challenge, but don't stop – you need to lead a 'normal' life at least some of the time if you are going to be able to maintain the strength you need. There will be times when you don't recognise your partner at all – when Bruce is in the middle of an episode it feels as if there is a glass wall between us – I can see and hear him, but there is nothing I can say or do that will register with him. And there have been times when medication has limited his life – keeping him out of hospital but making him too tired to engage fully in life. It's important to remember that the person you knew before diagnosis is still there, even when it doesn't feel that way.

There are no easy solutions for bipolar, but it is possible – with time, perseverance and determination – to manage it. You sometimes hear bipolar people say that if given the choice they'd keep it rather than lead their lives without it. I have always found this hard to understand, having seen first-hand the enormous challenges it presents. However, if Bruce wasn't bipolar, his life would most likely have taken a very different course, and we'd never have met. If he wasn't bipolar, some of the most exciting and formative experiences of our lives wouldn't have happened. Our lives would have both been very different, our three wonderful children wouldn't exist, and when times are tough, that's something worth remembering.

YOU ARE ONLY RESPONSIBLE FOR YOUR OWN HAPPINESS

by Liz Cain

I AM UNUSED TO WRITING non-fiction, so you might have to bear with me here. This is also hard for me to share, but I think it's important for anyone who feels the same way to know that you are not alone. The dark abyss of struggling for a way out of darkness doesn't last forever, even if sometimes it feels like it does. In sharing my story, I will be talking about my own personal experiences which could be confronting and triggering for any of you reading this who have had similar struggles. Thank you for reading my story, and if you feel triggered by anything please, please, don't be afraid to seek professional help.

Mental health has always been at the forefront of my mind. Having struggled with it one way or another since my early teens, it has been incredible to see the increased awareness in recent years. No longer do I have to worry about judgement or hear the phrase "I don't understand. Why don't you just get over it?" or "You have so much to be happy for. Why aren't you?"

I have had three points in my life where I have felt I hit rock bottom, each bad in their own way and usually a combination of what is happening in my life, as well as my own obsessive thoughts spiralling. Each was handled very differently when I sought the help and support that I desperately needed. From being dismissed as being overdramatic, to more awareness that mental health is a problem but still no help being provided, to still having to fight for support but finding that there is more tolerance for those with mental health issues.

I have had various diagnoses for my mental health issues. Depression, anxiety, stress. But I don't believe that any of these have in fact been true. I have been through several periods of turmoil in my life, and to be honest mental health has affected me in different ways depending on what has been happening around me. I prefer not to give it a label, as everyone who experiences issues with their mental health does so in a unique way. Looking back, I don't believe that I was depressed as a teenager. But being told repeatedly that there is something wrong with you and you should be happy, can make you start to believe what you're being told is true.

I was painfully shy as a teen, with very low self-esteem – which will be very hard to believe for anyone who knows me today. I was constantly bullied at school, which made me withdraw and never want to leave the house. School as a teenager can be brutal as I'm sure we all know. I don't like to think of those years and what I remember most is being alone, with no friends and looking forward to my escape when I left for university. Because then it would be different, wouldn't it?

It became a theme in my life that I would always look forward to the next stage, because then it would get better. It wasn't until my mid-twenties when I suddenly realised, I was wishing my life away and that wasn't acceptable. Being smart at our school was not something you could advertise. If you spoke out in class or answered questions when you were interested in the topic being discussed, then you learnt not to be alone in the corridor or restrooms. Being labelled smart was dangerous.

I remember having a horse-riding accident when I was fourteen and having eight weeks off school due to a broken arm. When I returned, I spent most days trying to think of a plausible way I could injure myself again so I could have more time off – home schooling had suited me well. But the concept of injuring yourself to avoid school and stay home is also a dangerous one to play around with.

I'm sure that a lot of people will agree when I say that there is nothing wrong with wanting to shut out the world and read a good book. I was particularly lucky when my parents moved us to a farmhouse in the country, in a small hamlet with a population of less than twenty people. Now I had an excuse to avoid people. The nearest bus stop was a mile away, the nearest village with a shop or pub was five miles and our nearest neighbour was a five-minute walk.

I lived with my parents and my two sisters; our family made up a large part of the hamlet's population and if we wanted to go anywhere, we had to be able to drive. Pretty hard when you're only twelve and must rely on your parents to take you anywhere. It also made it hard for friends to come over to your house to hang out – that was when I did have friends. Being so isolated though also made it hard for someone like me who was already inclined to avoid people, find the will to put myself out there and make new friends and acquaintances.

My friends became characters in books, and I started making up my own stories as an escape from a school I hated and living in an isolated area. I was perfectly happy with this situation in my early teens, but as I got older, I knew I would have to pass my driving test as soon as I could to gain any freedom. Around the age of fifteen I was encouraged by my school to join an athletics club as I had broken the triple jump record by over two metres.

I think I could write an entire book on the mental toll it takes to compete in sports. The best I achieved was representing the

North of England and ranking around eighteenth in the UK for women's triple jump. I admire anyone who has the ability to push through the mind games and self-doubt, and succeed in following their dream to take part in a sport they can enjoy. Needless to say, when I had the choice between continuing to pursue a career as an athlete and going to university, I chose university.

I am that annoying person who never really had to try at school to get good grades. Sorry Mum! When I said I was doing my homework and revising.... I really wasn't.

University was another story. There is certainly a large difference between A-levels and a degree. Saying that, I still managed to obtain a 2:1 without much more effort. Which is why it was a shock to my system when I was suddenly struggling to achieve the qualifications required in my professional career – I will cover this later.

Being one of three children can be difficult. I've never understood why parents choose to have three children. My husband and I are both one of three, and we both agree that at different times each child will feel left out. The eldest two will be close to begin with, as the youngest is still the baby, but as the eldest gets older and moves out the younger two become close.

I think it's safe to say that over the years, despite living with my middle sister twice since moving out of our parent's house, it was always me that felt left out. I still do some days as my parents moved south to be closer to both my sisters who now live in the same area as each other. Even though they only live a couple of hours away, it seems a lot further.

Now you may wonder what this has to do with mental health but support from your family is incredibly important. Their dismissal of your feelings, or inability to understand what you are going through can make everything a lot worse. I know my mum struggled, desperate to do anything to make things better. But being constantly fussed over, and your inability to pull yourself out of it being pointed out every day can make things worse. It can make you feel like a burden or that you don't deserve help because you aren't trying hard enough to be happy. That it is your fault that you feel the way you feel, and you need to "be happy".

I can assure you; it is not your fault! You are not a burden! I wish I could have told myself that on so many occasions. If only one person reads this and believes it then I will consider that a huge achievement. Your struggles are valid, and it's important to remember that struggling with mental health does not make you less. It does not take anything away from the person your friends and family love.

I started faking being ok around my family, masking my inner turmoil to get them off my back. Telling the doctors what they wanted to hear so I could come off my medication, telling my mum that I was fine and acting happy all the time. This in itself can add another dimension to anyone with mental health issues. The sheer exhaustion from having to pretend you are fine can be a deep, dark hole.

In my twenties, I found myself in a job I hated and continuing to fake my happiness at having a successful career. Fourteen to fifteen hours work a day due to staff shortages and lack of vacancies being filled causing further exhaustion. Most of the time I worked six days a week, having to get up at 5:30am to make it to work on time. During this period, I was expected to complete a training scheme to achieve the qualification I needed to be able to continue working in my profession. Without this I would have been asked to resign. When I did not achieve this qualification, disciplinary action was brought against me which resulted in extra stress at work and more pressure to complete my training within a short timeframe.

Long story short I took a leave of absence, signed off with stress for three months. Something had to give, and I was lucky that my doctor was willing to give me a sick note at the time. I will add that at this point when the three months was over, nothing had changed, and my doctor decided that I should be over it by now so I should go back to work. I am grateful that now it is more appreciated that mental health issues can become long term.

During my leave of absence, I attended mandatory counselling, and having never had counselling before I didn't know what to expect. I guess it helped. I don't really remember. I gained coping mechanisms that helped me get through each day. Or at least that is what I was told. I took their word for it as I can't remember what they were. Instead, I developed a very unhealthy relationship with alcohol as it was the only way I could get any sleep at night. Drinking was also a way to drown out all those overwhelming thoughts and feelings that I was struggling with.

Some days I felt too much, every emotion was overwhelming and physically painful. Other days I felt nothing, and those days were worse in their own way. Returning to that job was one of the hardest days of my life. I clearly remember the pressure weighing down on me, threatening to crush me as I walked down the long corridor to the open-plan office I shared with the rest of the department.

I wanted to get in there, keep my head down and get on with what I needed to do. Getting through one day at a time. But every step was a gauntlet. I work in an extremely specialised field, one in which there are very few jobs which come up each year. How I wish

I had discovered writing then as an outlet, I do wonder how things would have turned out if I had.

Writing is more than reading was to me, more than an outlet and an escape. It has become a joy, a way for me to release those feelings I hold in until I can't take it anymore. In my debut series, co-authored with a good friend, there is a line that appears in every book.

One step at a time.

This is a tribute to how I cope with my mental health issues, when everything is overwhelming me and it's all too much.

I take a moment to break everything I need to do down into a list. And I choose one step to take. When that is done, I choose another. Knowing that I can get through it, if I achieve one step at a time. This came from walking down that corridor, where every step was an achievement. By taking things one step at a time, it helped me break down the overwhelming sense of dread. The hyper focus on moving one foot in front of the other, allowed me to worry less about what my colleagues may be doing or saying around me.

Over the next eighteen months I had twelve job interviews, which went well but all had the same outcome. I got great feedback but kept hearing the phrase I didn't want to hear.

"We just can't take you on until you're qualified."

Whether it was my own determination or whether the coping mechanisms helped, I managed to gain the qualification I needed by taking annual leave and using my free time to do the work I needed to do; to submit the required evidence. This gave me the freedom to apply to other jobs in the same field, away from the place of work I hated and the area I lived in. Sadly, this area is now where my sisters and parents live and it can be daunting heading back to where I feel I hit the lowest point in my life.

The day I received the qualification, I applied for a job located within an hour of where I grew up. Away from the area I hated and back to a part of the country I loved. The North! I nearly backed out of the interview when I was asked to give a presentation as part of it. I still struggled with my confidence, but I pulled up my big girl pants and managed to smash the interview. No longer would I hear that dreaded phrase. Now that I had the qualification, I was immediately offered the job.

At the time, I had just started dating my now husband. He is the older brother of someone I went to school with and was in the same Form Room as me. My husband's brother was a fellow victim of the bullies, who also spent most days trying hard not to draw their attention. While we reminisced over escaping that hellhole, his older brother caught my eye. It was only by chance we ended up in the same pub when I was visiting my parents and we both are grateful that we happened to be in the same place at the same time.

When I got the job in Leeds, we were in that awkward phase where you aren't sure if it will be serious, but I think we both knew that if I didn't move closer then we weren't going to last. Now I can hear you all thinking, "Why couldn't he move closer to you?" That would be because I hated where I lived, and I'd been waiting for a job to come up near my hometown for six years. I wanted to be closer to where he already lived and worked. I'd say it worked out well even though I'm still an hour away from there.

As my grandmother always told me, I never *do anything by halves*. I never made things easy for myself. The weekend I moved three hours north of where I lived, I had three concerts in Nottingham, Wolverhampton, and Leeds to see three of my favourite bands – all in the same weekend. Tickets I'd had booked since the month before I applied to the job. I did what I normally do and stuck my head in the sand, hoping that it would all work out. Thankfully it did and I successfully moved into a flat, sometimes things can really fall into place.

It is incredible how when you have mental health issues, if you have someone who listens and doesn't try to fix you, listens but doesn't try to solve your problems and someone who is just there for you, it can make a huge difference in how you cope. It helped that at this point in my life I had been through my darkest moments and brought myself through to the other side on my own. But it was certainly easier having someone I could trust and lean on. My husband admits that he's never had mental health issues and can't understand what I'm going through. But he has never let me down or made me feel like it is my fault. He has been my rock, providing that quiet unconditional support that I have needed to pull myself back to some semblance of me.

I knew that I had been through worse and survived, so I would survive what comes next. No matter what it is. Saying that to myself has got me through some hard times, especially during COVID when it felt like we had one incident after another. I have become very good at absorbing stress over the years, absorbing the feelings I don't want to feel, but there is only so much a person can take. If I hadn't had the experience of the issues I'd suffered earlier in my life, then I would have broken down a lot earlier.

I won't say too much about what happened as I'm aware I'm on a limited word count. However, COVID wasn't even the hardest challenge we had to cope with over the last few years which is saying something. At the time, I did not feel strong. I felt like a failure. I wanted to scream at the world for how unfair life could be. Why can't I have anything easy? Why as soon as I feel happy does something happen to drag me backwards?

WRITING IS OUR SUPERPOWER

What doesn't kill you makes you stronger.

I have always thought it would be more accurate to say that it isn't whatever has broken you that makes you stronger. It is you. When a chair is broken, you can't put it back together and expect to sit on it without it breaking again. You must put the time in to fix it. Whether you use wood glue or screw it back together, you need to find the tools and learn how to reinforce the part that was broken. You might need to ask for help or do research to see how you can fix the chair. But it is your actions that put you back together again and make you stronger.

You only get one shot at life; it is your decision how you take the actions needed to ensure you are happy with it. I know how hard it can be to ask for help, I'm incredibly stubborn and have always struggled; believing I absolutely had to do everything by myself. It takes some learning. But when you do learn to ask for help, from the right people I might add, it's a game changer.

I have made the mistake of trusting the wrong person multiple times in my life and ended up having to leave behind some very toxic people. I could write another essay on the events that occurred and how people have taken advantage of my willingness to give large parts of myself to help others. I still feel guilty, as if I've abandoned them in some way and I'm not there to help them when they need me. Letting go of toxic thoughts can often take longer than the act of ridding yourself of the toxic individuals, but you must let them both go.

Even though I'm sure they don't even remember who I am anymore. I was someone to be used and discarded when they didn't need me. I have been much happier since letting those people go. I am not responsible for their happiness; this is my life and I'm responsible for my own happiness. That doesn't mean treating others unkindly or ignoring those in pain. It means putting on your own oxygen mask before helping others. And making sure that you're surrounding yourself with the right people.

Every mental health journey is different for each individual. This is my story and if it helps one person overcome their struggle, then mission accomplished. My journey has taught me how to recognise what a real friend is, what that friendship should look like. My struggles have also taught me how to distance myself from toxic relationships and those people that really don't care about me or anything outside of their self-centred worlds. No matter how hard that might be.

How you feel is how you feel. You are only responsible for your own happiness, and it is only you who can ensure it. Life is too short to make yourself miserable to make others happy. Especially if they don't notice or even care. This was a hard lesson for me to learn but once I did, I never looked back. Be careful with those who treat you badly, those who guilt you into giving yourself to them when they won't value it or you.

And when it is hard, remember to take a deep breath, put one foot in front of the other and take things one step at a time.

THE SILENCE IS DEAFENING

by Anonymous

Dance like nobody's watching,
sing like nobody's listening,
and write like nobody's reading

Before

GUILT. IT'S AN INSIDIOUS EMOTION that eats at our souls and ignores all reason. This story is not about logic but rather, the absence of it. My actions and reactions may not make sense to you and for a person without the shroud of depression, will be difficult to comprehend.

Let me rewind.

Seventeen years ago, I married the love of my life—my soulmate and best friend. Life was good. My heart was full.

Sixteen years ago, I gave birth to my daughter who deserved my love, my devotion, my heart.

That was the first warning sign. After thirty-seven hours of labour, she entered this world not screaming like most babies, but blue and unresponsive. I had failed in my first task as a mother. I should have *pushed harder and faster* to avoid her traumatic entry into the world. The instant bond and love that people write prose about, didn't exist.

Fifteen years ago, I knew something was wrong with her, so I sought the advice of my doctors. I was told it was teething—three times. She stopped breathing. Again, I should have *pushed harder and faster* to avoid lifelong complications.

Fourteen years ago, I learned I had a genetic disorder, a fatal one if not treated. If I have passed this on, I have failed.

Thirteen years ago, I was diagnosed with Trigeminal Neuralgia. A debilitating condition nicknamed 'the suicide disease'. This was the first time I stared at an open window from the fourth floor of a building and contemplated ending my life. It was a startling thought. Not a fleeting one, but a scary one, where I weighed the possibility of stopping the pain, the crippling guilt, the failure.

Fast forward.

My first brain operation cured the pain. It was like I could breathe again. But the recovery was tough. I lost six months to infections and exhaustion. You remember the height of Covid? Wash your hands regularly, take a shower if you've been with a group of people, antibacterial handles. If you feel unwell, isolate yourself. These were our house rules. We had no clue the damage we were causing our daughter.

The OCD started months later. She became increasingly reluctant to touch food, gained a pathological fear of becoming ill, and most tellingly, making me unwell. I should have seen it, I should have pushed *harder and faster* for help. I had failed.

The pain re-emerged two years later and with it, the guilt of knowing what was coming. The second brain operation cemented my daughter's OCD beliefs and began a period of psychosis. She regularly scalded her mouth and hands to deal with the germs. We grappled with recovery and an unwell daughter that was being given the run around by the mental health system. She wasn't deemed severe enough to warrant intervention.

This is where I began writing. I needed somewhere to pour my grief and anxiety. I needed a world I could control and be the master of my destiny. Characters that could go through Hell and survive.

My daughter's autism diagnosis came not long after. Research tells us it's linked to a traumatic birth or infection—everything that should have clued me into the struggles she was having navigating the world. As a mother, I had failed again.

Six months later, she admitted to me on the way home from school that she had made plans to take her life. I called for help, none came. I should have *pushed harder and faster.* I failed.

One week later, she took a blade to her legs for the first time. I bandaged her and the mental health system listened, but ultimately, pushed the responsibility back to us and this is where my story begins.

Then

HIGH FUNCTIONING DEPRESSION means to the outside world you seem okay. You go to your day job, you do all the tasks of a wife and parent, you even socialize. But on the inside, the cracks are starting to appear. Deep down, you know something is wrong, but the demands of the world mean you grin and bear it. You smile at the postman and nod when colleagues ask you for favours.

But every waking moment was guided by the fear of my daughter hurting herself. I was in a raised state of anxiety for months. I slept two, maybe three hours a night. I moved an extra bed into her room and held her when she wanted to die. When her chaotic world became too much, I became her shield. I cried in the shower every morning when no one could hear me and buried myself in more complex and demanding tasks at work to hide my crumbling mind.

Something had to give.

I'M AN EMOTIONAL person. I cry at movies, at charity adverts, at concerts—I wear my heart on my sleeve, much like my characters, and I'm not ashamed of it. I look for the good in everyone and forgive easily. I rarely hold a grudge and don't hang on to the past.

Which is why when I woke on the 20th June 2022, I had never been more terrified. I was numb, and my chaotic mind fell silent. An emptiness sat in the pit of my stomach, the tears had stopped, and the worry was gone. I drove to work and once there, couldn't remember a single thing about the journey. I held conversations with colleagues and even taught lessons, which I have no recollection of.

One insistent thought broke through the silence. I needed everything to stop.

Stop moving.

Stop hurting.

Stop fighting.

Stop breathing.

I felt like I had failed my daughter again and again.

For the sanity and health of my husband, my daughter, my colleagues even—I needed to no longer exist on this earth. There came a startling clarity that my death would better the world, that I was the cause of so much heartache and distress in my own home, and that without me, things would be better for everyone I love. This failure could stop.

I'm incredibly lucky to have a colleague who recognised the pain I was in and held my hand. As I reached out, I got help and I held on to the metaphors.

It will pass.

Keep breathing.

There's a light at the end of the tunnel.

Behind every rain cloud is the sun.

Now

THERE'S TRUTH IN all of this, but also something people don't feel comfortable telling you—it will pass, but you have to keep going in order to get through. No one can do that for you. You have to be strong to push on.

You have to breathe to live. But every single inhalation of air will drain you more than running a marathon. It's okay to be exhausted, you are in a constant battle with an invisible force that knocks you down every opportunity it gets.

In your darkest moments, the light at the end of any tunnel won't be visible, you'll question if it even exists, but you have to keep digging in the dirt. Your fingers will become raw and bloody, you will feel like giving up every single day. But if you dig long enough and hard enough, you will create your own light.

As for the rain, I've learned to dance in it and stop expecting the sunshine. I see the beauty in the storm as much as the sun.

Make no mistake, this is a war. A war with my own mind, and every day is a unique battle. Some days are easier than others. Recovery is not a linear process—it's not a case of getting a little better every day which is typical of physical injury. This is an injury to your soul, and just when you find something to cover one crack, the insidious thoughts break you apart in new and inventive ways.

You have to find something to get out of bed for. Something that doesn't judge you when all you managed was to brush your teeth or comb your hair. For me, that is writing. Has it been easy this last year? No, and I don't believe any author will tell you writing is easy. But there's something freeing in choosing which world to immerse myself in today and knowing I'm bringing those words to life for readers who may be fighting a battle of their own, whether that be a mental or physical one.

I doubt I will ever be the person I once was, and there's a part of me that mourns for the me of before. It's similar to grief, I've not lost a loved one, but rather myself. I worry that family and friends won't understand that she isn't coming back, that I will lose them when they realize the woman they loved no longer exists.

I've lost friends. People who I thought would be with me through thick and thin. It's a rejection that stings, because for some, if you can't be that happy dependable person people have always known, then they are no longer interested. It's taken time, but I've realized that's okay. They didn't sign up for my breakdown, and while it stung, I no longer hurt.

On the flip side, I've opened my heart and found a hugely supportive community in the book world. I have made lifelong friends, people who will always pick me up when I fall. Who will dust me off and encourage me to keep waking up, keep writing, keep breathing. Many of these people don't know my personal story, but it doesn't matter, they show up. Every. Single. Day.

Some days, the silence is still deafening, but with time, those days are lessening. I will beat this and continue to pick up my pen because writing is my superpower, and if my characters bring light to just one person, then it is worth it.

Playlist & Explanation

Visiting Hours - Ed Sheeran
I partly lived with my grandmother until I was sixteen. At age nineteen, she died very suddenly. I truly wish my daughter could have met her, and that I could ask her advice on everything that has happened.

Daylight - Shinedown
In November 2022, I attended a concert and this song, the lyrics, the pain—it absolutely broke me into pieces with its truth.

What I Know So Far - Pink
A ballad to my daughter for better times.

To my beautiful friend
Thank you for being you
Love you lots Paula xx

"DRINK YOUR JUICE, PAULA!"

by Paula Ramsden

CLOSE YOUR EYES AND IMAGINE you are in a circus tent. You're riding a unicycle, trying your hardest to keep your balance, when suddenly you are asked to juggle some balls too! You start with three, then people in the crowd throw more at you. The spotlight is always on and you are trying to balance on the unicycle, but the balls keep dropping, you have to keep stopping, get off the unicycle, pick them up, get back on and start again. The crowd keeps throwing more balls and you keep trying your best but somehow it is never good enough. You can feel the anger and frustration building and you have nowhere to turn. You fall and collapse in a heap utterly exhausted.

What I have described in the circus scene above may sound extreme but let me break it down. The unicycle is just the usual daily routine of get up, get dressed etc. The first lot of balls are again things most people have to do: sort kids out, plan the meals, go to work, walk the dogs, cook the meals, clean the house, go shopping... you get my drift. Now the extra balls that keep getting thrown are all my diabetic crap. Prepare yourself as this list is endless! Monitor blood sugars, adjust insulin accordingly – has it been adjusted right? Will my blood go down or up? How many carbs are in that packet of crisps? Have I got orange juice in my bag? Have I got spare infusion sets or spare batteries? Is today the day I collapse again?

So, welcome to my world. The one that changed at eleven years old. Overnight, I had to become a scientist and mathematician responsible for whether I lived or died. I had to come to the realisation that I had to inject myself with something that "normal people" create themselves – and even a drop of what I was injecting could kill a normal person.

I have been a Type 1 diabetic for 33 years and I have had "official" diabetic burnouts on three occasions. However, most of the time I try to hide how I am feeling and stick a smile on my face and try to deal with it the best I can.

How do I explain a diabetic burnout? That is a hard question to answer as, like most illnesses, they affect people differently, but here goes...

I am constantly feeling a high level of stress and anxiety. I have this persistent thought that even after 33 years (and improvements in technology), that if my blood is high, then I'm going to die, and if my blood is low, then I'm going to die. There is no in-between and I am constantly battling this in my head. Every time I scan my arm to take a blood glucose reading (I'm one of the lucky ones who has a sensor and a pump, but believe me, I have had to fight every step of the way to get them), I feel sick and full of dread knowing that if it's not perfect the nurses can see it (they have access to my glucose levels remotely 24/7) and I will be questioned even though sometimes, I have no control over it and no idea why it's happened. I can be 100% perfect, have worked out all my carbs to insulin ratios, have exercised, but bloods still are not in the normal range. I then think back to what I have done wrong, making me stressed which, yep, you have guessed it, affects my blood sugars.

Then having to remember to test my blood, make sure I have enough insulin in my pump to get me through the day especially if

I'm out and about, making sure I have spare diabetic stuff. Keeping track of what I have eaten, what I have done. Remembering what appointments I have coming up, and do I need a "fasting" blood test or just a normal sample?

Feeling like this day in, day out is exhausting – having to justify myself to family, friends, doctors and consultants. Feeling worthless and that nothing I do is good enough and that in the end, what is it all for...? I might still go blind, might lose my toes, my legs, my kidneys, might still slip into a diabetic coma when no one is home. Am I just prolonging all of this? I am never going to be free of this disease, so what is the point!

You might have guessed by now that I also suffer from depression linked to diabetic burnouts. What might surprise you is that compared to the public, diabetics are more than twice as likely to commit suicide and inflict self-harm.

That might be shocking to you but for me, I get it. What I wouldn't give to be "normal" for just one day, eat what I want, exercise if I want to (without having to adjust insulin rates, then have orange juice after to boost sugars). I want to go out without packing spare infusion sets, insulin vials, batteries, insulin pens, needles, glucose tablets. What would it be like to be free?

I think I am one of the lucky ones. I have an amazing family who have been there since day one helping me through it. I will always remember getting ready for school with my dad sat in the armchair, me eating my breakfast in total silence. Everyone knew not to speak to me before I'd had my morning injection!

Not sure how my parents coped through my teenage years as I was a bugger, going clubbing at fourteen, staying out etc. I honestly think that by allowing me to just get on with it, they have allowed me to live and made sure I enjoyed those years. However

I know that they worried every time I went out and I also know that they still do. My mum only stopped coming to my diabetic appointments with me when I got married. Although I was never allowed to watch *Steel Magnolias* for obvious reasons (spoiler, the diabetic dies). I watch it now and it still makes me cry. Side note, I really want a t-shirt that says "Drink your juice, Shelby" as that sums up my life!

My husband is amazing. I'm not sure he signed up for the crap that comes with loving me but my god has he been there every step of the way. His first experience of me, my diabetes and the complications it causes was during sex. Have you ever had to stop and ask for some orange juice and a Kit Kat? I have and it brings a whole new meaning to their slogan, "Have a break, have a Kit Kat!"

The second and hardest time of our life was being told we couldn't have children due to PCOS related to diabetes. He came home one night to me in the lounge crying, surrounded by filled insulin syringes ready to end it. He sat with me all night, holding me and crying with me. The next day, I was put on happy pills (the first of many times). All this led to tests, sex diaries, endless appointments, being told what to eat, what not to eat, blood tests and endless tears. We went through hell and although we have two angel babies, we are still the lucky ones as we also have two beautiful daughters.

The stress and anxiety of being pregnant was immense. I cried scared tears rather than happy tears when I found out. We had baby scans every fortnight, and I got told if I didn't do things right, my actions could damage the baby. I ended up putting on nearly eight stone when pregnant so I was very thankful for our amazing NHS.

I feel bouts of guilt when I look back to when the girls were younger. We put pictures up and the numbers to call an ambulance, my mum or my husband in case anything should happen to me and the children needed to call someone. My eldest used to have tea parties with her teddies and she would pretend to inject them after they had finished eating their cake. To them it was a normal part of growing up, to me it just added to the mummy guilt, the stress and the anxiety.

Work life is another area where I struggle. When your blood is low, you are shaking, sweating, you can't form a sentence and you need sugar at that moment regardless if you are in a meeting, on a phone call or just sitting at the desk. I have worked with some great people who could spot the signs and made me eat and drink ... did I mention I can get quite stubborn too?

I once collapsed whilst in Sainsbury's in my lunch hour. On that day I had tested my blood and it was high, my pump worked out the correct dose, I pressed the button on the pump, job done. Or so I thought. I woke up surrounded by bottles of shampoo and conditioner, on the floor, in a puddle of my own pee. I was taken to hospital to get checked over but all was fine. What did I do wrong? I honestly don't know, but my eyes were going funny, like watching an old black and white movie with all the blinking from scene to scene. I now know this is a sign of low blood sugars, but there are so many unique symptoms and it's not as straightforward as you might think.

This has happened on a few occasions, either at home or work. One was on the way to Occupational Health to discuss my absence. You really couldn't have made it up!

When I wake up from a fit, my whole body hurts; my muscles are so stiff due to becoming rigid. I have normally bitten my tongue and the insides of my mouth and I will have a huge bump somewhere on my head and a nice arrangement of bruises. It takes about a week to heal but mentally I don't think I will ever heal. I have a tattoo on my wrist stating that I am a Type 1 diabetic as it got to the stage where I didn't want to go out on my own. I gave up running as I was so scared of collapsing. The tattoo has given me back some of my confidence.

The result of a "normal" hypo is tiredness; it feels like I have the biggest hangover ever. I just want to curl up in bed, yet I get up and carry on like all is fine – after all, it was only a low blood sugar at 3am, right?!

Driving is another area that for diabetics causes a lot of high anxiety – well for me anyway! By law you are not allowed to drive if your blood is lower than 5.7 (normal blood for a non-diabetic is 6.5). So what happens if I am in a rush, do my blood and it is lower than that, and I get in the car and have an accident? The police will review my meter/sensor, find my reading and I will be done for dangerous driving. So I have to allow myself enough time to be able to neck some orange juice and wait for my blood to rise before driving. A total pain in the arse but really not worth the risk to myself and other road users.

Every three years I have to renew my driving licence with DVLA and I have to give them permission to review my medical information. They check that I have had my eye screenings, diabetic checks and no loss of consciousness within the past three years. I had my licence taken off me for eighteen months after my first fit and then I got pregnant. The DVLA, with help from my consultant, would not reissue my licence until my daughter was six months old. That was a very stressful and upsetting time and I absolutely dread when that DVLA letter hits the doormat. Just another ball to juggle!

For me having a doctor who understands and recognises a diabetic burnout has been the best. Without her I would still be standing on the edge of the black hole, waiting to jump in and disappear, just to get away from the daily crap I have to do.

I would love to see a cure in my lifetime, not for me – it would make my diabetic tattoo pointless! But for that scared eleven-year-old girl, on Halloween, crying, sat in a hospital bed, listening to the other kids at the Halloween party, being told that she can't have ice cream.

That girl who is unsure what's really happening, being shown how to inject herself, meanwhile her parents are trying to be strong knowing that all their lives are going to change and nothing will ever be the same again.

The one good thing about that night is that my aunt gave me tickets to see Jason Donovan, in the flesh, on a skateboard! See, good things do come out of being ill!!!

So that's a whistlestop tour of diabetes and diabetic burnout! This isn't a "woe is me" piece – this is my life and just a small fraction of what I go through every day and night. If you know anyone who is diabetic, please reach out to them as the mental impact is huge. Just please don't ever say the following things:

"Is your blood low?" when they are moody, snapping, emotional, look pale. Nine times out of ten it will be, but it drives me and almost all the diabetics I know, mad!

"You don't look ill." Whoa, totally the wrong thing to say to someone who has had to get up at 3am to down a shit load of orange juice!

"Diabetes in a cup or on a plate." (When referencing a sugar-filled treat you're having or have seen – donuts, chocolate etc). For Type 1 diabetics it really isn't! I was eleven and they think it was

the shock of my grandparents dying close together that triggered it. Most people can eat as much crap as they want and won't develop it. I get so cross with this one so excuse me while I step down from my soap box......

For more information on diabetes and diabetic burnout visit www.diabetes.org.uk

For information on insulin pumps visit www.medtronic.com

POETRY & PROSE CAN HEAL THE PAIN

by Audrina Lane

I GUESS PEOPLE WHO KNOW me, know I always have a smile on my face. They would be right, but a smile can also be the best place to hide when things are not going well.

When I think back, my first bout of depression was when I was 17 years old. My first relationship had been ended by him and I felt like my heart had been torn in two. I read a powerful poem for my English A-Level and it struck a chord. Perhaps I should end things now in a nice warm bath with a knife at my wrist, I thought. This image gnawed away at me for months as I carried on with my life. However, I wrote a poem called *Knife* and then a year later, wrote the first draft of what was to eventually become my first novel, *Where Did Your Heart Go?* but at the time was called *Take My Breath Away*. My dark monster moved away as I wrote the very scene I was imagining, but fear and doubts about my writing in the early 1990s meant I put my manuscript into a box file and left it in the attic.

Fast forward to 2015 and I was working for Herefordshire Council running what had been the Mobile Library Service but with the closure of that turned into a home delivery service. Times were hard for public services, we were forever being told to save money, make cuts and that our whole service was under threat. I had a team of five, previously nine, a huge workload and was in turn supporting some of my staff with their own personal issues.

That was when the bullying started. A senior manager started on two different members of my team and then me. Always she kept the comments and accusations to when any of us were alone with her. She eroded my sense of self-confidence and worth. She was not my line manager, as she had the same line manager as me. Following procedure, I went to him with mine and my staff's bullying issues. He promised to investigate but then he ended up being off with stress and mental health issues – and who was handed his workload? You guessed it, the woman in question.

It truly felt like we were all fighting a losing battle! The dark thoughts arrived again as an anonymous person accused me of various bad practices and I was under investigation and told to remain silent. Even turning to the union I was a member of was no use, she was a union rep and no one wanted to go up against her. I really understood the proverb about being stuck between a rock and a hard place. There seemed no way to escape, not even higher management listened. My dark thoughts returned and in my mind I would dream. There was a sharp turn on my way home from work, what if I just floored the car at that point and crashed over the edge? I dreamed about it every night, even imagining that my partner and my dogs were in the car with me. That I couldn't bear to leave them so they would have to come with me.

But what if I failed, what if they died and I lived or I died and they were left. This whole jumble of thoughts forever running through my head. I tried to open up to my partner, but he told me that I was being over dramatic about what was happening at work and that if I was a stronger manager, or person, I could cope with the stress. So, I hid it all from him, too. Once again, a smile on my face to hide behind, a mask of my own creation to keep prying eyes at bay because I knew I would crack, I would splinter.

The only thing that kept me sane, because I didn't think the anti-depressants I was prescribed were working, were words. My poetry in particular can take a dark and miserable side. It is like I pour all the feelings of despair into them. One of my darkest ones is this, it highlights how the depression was colouring my belief in my relationship:

Suffocation
I beat the invisible bars
I scream silently
Trapped in this mire
Of suffocating love
Gasping and breathless
You will not let me expand
I have to conform
To your control
I want to spread my wings
Emerge from the chrysalis
That binds me
To your will
My creativity is stifled
The page is blank
Empty
Like my heart
That was once filled with love
For you
Until you changed me
Or did I change you?

And this one I think really talks about how physical depression can feel:

Ripples
Dropping through
The glassy, calm surface
Cold and icy
Leaving ripples
Ever expanding
Before disappearing
Pale Blue
Dark Indigo
Deep Black
All the shades between
Before darkness
No light from above
None from below
How deep will I fall?

Once again, words and my writing took away the power of the dark thoughts, even though it took a career change to really banish them.

My most recent dances with depression came in 2020 and 2021. I worked through Covid in the environment that the news was saying was the worst place to be, a Nursing Home. I watched as a new company took over at the home where I worked. When the crisis hit, they seemed to have no clue, no PPE, and most frightening of all, no care or compassion. I was not a carer just an Activity

Co-ordinator who was trying her best to keep the spirits of the residents high. A new manager said that I didn't need to wear a mask, so I took my own in to work. Once more a bully had come into my working life and my spirit started to crumble as I passed the rooms of residents dying from Covid. Some even called my name but I wasn't allowed to enter. As each of them passed away I poured my sadness into tribute poems about their lives, it was the only way I could cope.

Then in 2021 came a family crisis that floored me. My younger sister was diagnosed with oesophagus cancer and it had progressed so fast, it was Stage 3 and was in the lymph nodes to her lungs. She rang me and my other younger sister to tell us that she was having palliative care and that she had to make memories. I was the eldest, I had to be the strongest for all of them, I felt the huge burden of also helping my parents. How could life have dealt this death sentence to my sister, my younger sister, my sister who had three children and grandchildren, my sister who at the time was facing her scariest moment. It felt like sheer hell and I was a helpless feather in the centre of a wild tornado. This time my writing did stop, words seemed frivolous when believing we had just months to stay as the family we were. But my sister stayed strong and fought. She was young enough to withstand the toughest cure and thankfully it worked. Or at least she is currently in the clear.

For those who are reading this and have read my novels, you may see signs of all my struggles from the past in the pages you read. Maybe when you read them you didn't realise it was so biographical. So maybe they don't all have a traditional Happy Ever After, but who can say that their life has turned out that way? No one can see the future and I don't know when the darkness might catch up with me again, but if anything, the last couple of years have shown me that life is not a given and you should make the absolute most of what you have.

Anyone out there who suffers or has suffered from depression, anxiety, self-doubt. Please try and stay strong, find the crutch that will get you through and never be afraid to ask for help.

SPLIT

by Anonymous

These words are selfish, and personal, and, after many years trying to cope or find mechanisms for coping, I've found that sometimes selfishness is not a bad thing.
In fact, it's necessary for your own mental wellbeing.
Let me start at the beginning...

I THINK I WAS ABOUT nine when I realised something was wrong at home. I was loved, I knew that, but my father was difficult. Mum managed him as best as she could, and she loved him despite his faults. And I loved him, too. But it became more and more difficult at home. He couldn't cope with a growing young girl who began answering back, and he didn't know how to deal with the full force of actual family life either. I know it was worse than a young me remembers, and I'm sure I've buried some of the things I do remember because I just don't want to. Things like domestic violence and affairs.

Eventually, after endless screaming and shouting and wrongdoings on his part, plus his lack of will to provide for his family and the constant pressure on Mum and home life and me crying, she asked him to leave. He did. I say asked – I'm not sure it was that nice.

After he'd gone, and I tried to find my way through that, I thought the house would be calmer. It was for a time. Mum worked her fingers to the bone to provide everything the house needed, and she worked even harder to give me the things that she knew I wanted. And let's not forget the normal keeping up with the Joneses – the trainers, the right jeans, the right coat and bag etc. Somehow, she managed with a smile on her face. But he'd come back on and off, and, in the process, he made both our lives seem on edge constantly. He seemed to think that even though he'd gone, and that he didn't provide anything for us, we were still his in some way.

Something about that time, or perhaps the initial time of living with him or various other things, changed my mum. She started crying – a lot. She struggled with everyday things, and, after a time, she became a shell of who she'd been to me. Every morning she'd cry, and every night she'd cry. She'd get snappy for no reason, or we'd end up arguing about things that didn't need arguing about – in my mind, anyway. And slowly I started to think it was me – that it was my fault. And even if it wasn't my fault, I didn't seem to be able to do anything to make it better. In fact, the thought struck that if I wasn't there then Mum wouldn't have all those things to provide. I'm sure you know where that led my head to.

That's when the pressure really started kicking in for me.

You see, mental health wasn't really a thing back then, and it certainly wasn't something a twelve/thirteen-year-old girl knew anything about. All I saw was a desperately unhappy woman who was supposed to be my mum. She was supposed to be there for me, and she was supposed to be this endless line of support. That's what parents are, right? And my father was gone so she was the only one left. It was her job to be okay, to look after me, to be there if I had problems and if I needed help. And she did. Don't get me wrong, she tried, despite her problems, but somehow, over time, not only did I become the one who needed to support her, I also became the reason for all her problems. Stupid really, because there wasn't much I could do about any of it, and being alive wasn't my fault, but stuff like that doesn't make sense to a young girl. So, the only thing I could do was learn to not give her anything more to worry about.

I don't really remember those years clearly, and I know I did have fun. She did support me in things, and she'd drive me anywhere and try getting money together to make sure I got to do the things I needed to do. I had friends over all the time, possibly because she knew that made it easier for me and took the weight of me off her. We went on holidays. We laughed. But through all that time, there was still the constant edge of fear in me – what is she going to be like this morning, or this evening, or tomorrow? We'd have a great day. And then we'd have awful days. Those were the days that seemed to last for months. And then we'd have time where everything was okay again for a while.

And then it would go bad. Really bad.

IT DOESN'T SOUND like a lot, and it's hard to explain, but that continual pressure on a child – day in, day out – takes root and means a coping mechanism begins to form. I suppose those mechanisms come in many forms for different people, but for me it hardened me. It made me less empathetic to anything that could potentially cause me pain – or so I thought. I learned to numb myself to her crying because, well, nothing I did made it any better, and no amount of me making suggestions or trying to offer solutions made the problem go away. It was just the same continual cycle of mental pain for her. And that pain seemed to come and go at will, and then spiral her further down into an unknown hole that she couldn't, or didn't want, to claw herself out of.

I want to make a clear point here: I was in pain, too. That's important to recognise. I didn't at the time. I didn't understand what I was doing to myself, or how my coping mechanism was spiralling me towards a different direction, but my only way of seeing sense and not being pulled down into the same hole as her was to harden up. Ignore it. I suppose I chose to find a new route so I never had to deal with that pain again. Selfish perhaps, but back then I just did what I had to do. Let's just add in the fact here that my father was pretty much gone by this point, and he only came back every now and then as if our relationship should be somehow okay despite his almost disappearance from my life. As far as I was concerned at the time, he had no rights whatsoever in my life. None. He abandoned me because he couldn't cope, and potentially caused the problem I was left having to deal with – as a child. He put everything on my mum to deal with, basically told me I was unwanted by his actions, and then had the audacity to come back and pretend it was okay? Yeah, I was really angry with him. There was no forgiveness or tolerance inside me for him.

I wondered, often, if I'd wake up one morning and find her dead.

Or if I'd come home from school and find her in a pool of vomit from an overdose.

I knew about suicide and went to sleep on those thoughts.

And I kept wondering, all the time, what I could do to help – to make it better.

Nothing, was the answer.

Absolutely nothing.

The trouble was that my coping mechanism was turning me into someone who was practical rather than compassionate. I didn't want to listen to endless words from friends about how they were feeling, or why they felt the way they did. I couldn't understand the need for people to constantly go over the same ground time and time again, with no clear plan or direction to try leading themselves out of the hole they were falling into. And worse, I didn't want to. The action plan in my head was always aimed at 'where is the route out of this'. People who couldn't recognise that path incensed me. It isn't that I was completely unsympathetic to the trauma or problem a person was dealing with, but I lost sympathy for rehashing it over and over and over again. What was the point? Did that solve anything? Make it better? No. I'd learned that the hard way already. All it offered was an endless 'woe is me' tale that didn't get anyone anywhere other than more tears.

And through that time, Mum still wasn't right and I found myself unable to cope.

What did I do? See above. Action plan:

I finished my college course. Got my degree and applied for jobs.

And I left home at seventeen and moved a few hours away.

I want to make clear here that Mum was better in some ways by now. She'd seen doctors and had been given medication to help. It did work on some levels. It minimised some of the uncertainty with anxiety and depression, and gave her hope of less debilitating effects. But still, for me, it was broken at home. Or maybe I was. Not sure. I'm still working on that. But, either way, I'd become someone who couldn't live calmly with that uncertainty in my life, despite my love for her or my need to still try making it better. My mind, in fact, my whole being needed space from it. I was selfish. I had to be. I couldn't live with the pressure anymore, or understand why I should.

The guilt that hit me in that first year away from home was horrendous. I struggled with my new life regardless of loving it. I struggled to feel like I deserved any freedom from that energy I'd grown up in. Mainly because I knew she was still going through it, and I felt like I'd abandoned her when she needed me. I knew what feeling abandoned felt like. My father had done it to me.

I used to think of her crying and suffering at home without me. I'd go out and have a good time, and then, when I got back to my house and smiled about some joke or fun thing that had happened, I'd remember her sitting there: Miserable. Alone. Possibly contemplating whether she should bother waking up tomorrow.

I can't tell you how much that hurt.

I'm tearing up now I'm thinking about it again.

And did I call her to check in? Not always. I tried to live without that pressure guiding me, all the time wondering: is her pain mine to bear, too? Should I really be back there with her rather than living my life and enjoying it? Who said it was okay for me to be okay when she wasn't?

I needn't have felt that way. Mum certainly wouldn't have wanted me to feel like that, but I did anyway. And every time I saw her – no matter her mental state at the time - guilt hit again. I might not have shown it, and still don't to this day really, but it was there. It's been a constant in my life for all kinds of things that weren't mine to feel guilty about. It carried on for the next few years at that job, and then followed me into the next. So, guess what I did – I hardened further. I closed down to anything that might hurt my heart strings, while still trying to find out who I was, what I wanted out of life, and what type of people I wanted to be around.

The main thing I got wrong through all that time? I didn't recognise that her mental pain was not mine to carry. Probably because I still wanted to help somehow, and knew I couldn't. That's a problem with mental health, it infects everything and everyone around it, and makes everyone question everything about how feelings should feel.

YEARS ROLLED ON. I had relationships that didn't work – like everyone does – and I began to question why. Was I too hard on people? Did I not listen enough? Was I now so hardened that I didn't give people's emotional state the time it deserved? Possibly all of the above, but I wasn't about to let any barrier down until I'd understood why I'd put it there in the first place. I mean, what conversations did deserve time versus the pointless words that got people nowhere and didn't offer a way out of the problem? None of it made any sense to me at that time. I was just there to live life and enjoy it. I certainly wasn't ready to give someone a chance at touching my heart strings if the potential consequence was me either being hurt or abandoned. Emotive conversation cut way too close to the bone, on too many levels.

You see, conversation about emotions brought back the worst memories. They were all based in tears and pain. My mum's pain. My pain. Maybe even my father's pain, not that I knew what that could possibly have been. They made me think about feelings I hadn't dealt with. Feelings of being abandoned and abandonment. In fact, any talk that might prove emotional became a guilt trip for me. Because, for some bloody reason in my head, it was always my job to make it better and possibly my fault. So if I didn't listen to it, I wouldn't have to make it better or feel guilty about whose fault it was. I wouldn't need to feel that person's pain, nor would I have to make a plan and try endless ways to find a route through it – for them.

It wasn't that I didn't want to make it better, I did. But, unfortunately, I tried making it better a long time ago, and nothing ever made it better – especially when people didn't act. And when you see people not acting time and time again, and you watch the same thing destroying their mental wellbeing time and time again, what's the point of putting any effort into helping them?

Especially when it destroys your own mental health.

Somehow, my head had decided that it was easier to let other people deal with their own stuff.

Simpler.

For me, at least.

MORE YEARS PASSED by, and, by now, Mum was better to a degree. She had a new partner who supported her in every way. He let her be as she needed to be. She wanted to cry? He held her. She had a panic attack about doing something? He did it for her. She wanted to just be left alone? He left her alone. He was everything my father wasn't, and he helped her in ways that I couldn't. He was selfless. Endlessly so. For her. He listened for hours and hours, letting her rehash things over and over again with no clear end in sight. He was wonderful. A beautiful human being.

Great, right?

Yes and no.

Because, you know what? It just made me feel worse somehow. Deep down it hurt that I couldn't do that for her. Fundamentally, I guess, I was a villain in my own eyes suddenly because someone had made it better. Whereas I'd hardened to the endless problem and abandoned her to get on with my own life. Where was that guilt level now? Sky high.

Years have gone by, and I'm still not sure where I am in my own mental state about the whole scenario. Things have changed for Mum. Advanced medication makes her so much better, but her partner died. We knew it was coming, and that added a new level of difficulty to her already fractured mental health. He did everything he could to make sure she'd be taken care of when he died, and part of that was moving them both closer to me. Support for her. A grandchild to get involved in. A life, you know? He was a beautiful human until the end, and it helped her become who she is today.

However, I'm still a little lost with what her mental health did, or still does, to me. My tolerance for anxiety and depression should be higher than most people's. I should listen to its loud voice when I hear it, but if anything, my patience for it is a burden that eats at me constantly even though I'm not the one with it. Every word that comes from the mouth of someone with anxiety and depression causes a reaction in me that is not healthy for me. It doesn't matter if they're in a bad place or not, because I'm waiting for the downwards spiral regardless. I'm analysing each sentence for insight, so I can prepare to harden again. I just seem to return to being twelve/thirteen/fourteen years old, and once again I'm wondering what I need to do to make it better.

And then I feel guilty about that for the rest of the day, week, month.

I think constantly about what could make it easier, or if me being part of the situation makes it harder for them. I think about how, perhaps, helping makes it worse because then that person isn't dealing with the problem themselves. I wonder if perhaps doing things for people with anxiety and depression just prolongs the problem and makes it continue on forever. Because if they don't find a way out of it themselves – a clear path to at least some freedom from it, or control over it, who can?

But that seems selfish – a way to run away from the pain I might feel.

So then I consider the balanced thought process that maybe it's best to just sit and listen, to not try to help, but just listen for an hour, two hours, three days, a month. To let them talk, cry, cling onto you for however long it takes, regardless of how much it takes out of you to hear someone else's pain. It won't hurt to do that, right? But I already know it does hurt. It really fucking hurts to watch someone you love go through something you can't do anything about.

I know years of that hurt.

So then the other thought process comes along. Is it everyone else's job to listen to endless pain? To absorb it constantly? Is someone else's mental health worth more than our own? How do we value whose mental state is most important? Where is the line? When does your own anxiety and mental wellbeing about a situation become more important than someone you care about?

THOSE LAST FEW paragraphs are why this piece is called *Split*. I am split. I have been for a very long time. I am rational and straightforward as a human being, perhaps self-forced that way. I am here to laugh and love and enjoy life, but I am also a mess of internal feelings that struggle to connect with each other. I have more empathy than most people, whether I show it or not. I feel, on a deep and constant level, everyone's pain. I cry, often, about how to make it better. And because I try to limit that empathy, I live with an ongoing guilt that consumes me in relationships and friendships. It's as if something inside seeks to tell me I'm wrong to live without other people's pain invading my relatively straightforward approach. It gnaws at me constantly, making sure that I allow other's pain into me regardless of there being a way out or not. Was that my upbringing's fault? Or did my coping mechanism create more of a problem than the original problem ever was to a young child? Did I suppress something that I should have run with?

I don't know.

The one thing I do know is that mental health needs discussing – for all involved. It can't be shut down. It doesn't just magically disappear. And it sometimes affects the ones who live around it in ways you'll never see. It might seem like there's nothing wrong with them in your eyes. They don't crumble or cry in front of anyone. They don't let it out. They're okay, right? They can take whatever life throws at them, so asking them to listen to problems shouldn't be an issue. Or maybe they're the type to become a wall of stone, seemingly unaffected by anything. They're the rock. The solid one. The one you can go to. But I can tell you now, if they're anything like me, they put up that façade so they don't put pressure on anyone or force their own pain into others. They choose to shield the ones they care about from their issues and deal with it alone. Perhaps they become a show. An unrealistic version of strength and happiness.

Perhaps they're the ones that need the support.

Not that they'd ever ask for it.

And maybe they don't deserve it, either.

SURVIVING MOTHERHOOD

by B Crowhurst

MOTHERHOOD. IT'S A CONCEPT WE'RE all familiar with. We all have mothers in our lives, whether they be our own or somebody else's. In fact, over 2 billion people on the planet are mothers. And yet, there is so much about becoming a mum that no one ever really talks about. Which is exactly why I want to talk about it.

I am Mum to two wonderful children, who are currently five and seven. My world starts and ends with them, and I wouldn't have it any other way. However, our life is not all picture-perfect days out and a home always filled with smiling, happy faces every day. *That's not reality.*

Unfortunately, we live in a world where social media would have us believe that *other* families are always happy, and that *other* mums still manage to do their hair and make-up every day and that *other* people's children sleep through the night and behave like angels. It took me a very long time as a new mum to realise that, despite what I scrolled through on social media every day, other people were in the exact same boat that I was and finding it just as hard sometimes. People tend to post only the best of themselves on social media, so you only see the five minutes where everyone was having a great time. What you don't see are the umpteen tantrums, explosive nappies, spoilt dinners, and tears on the bathroom floor that more than likely came before and after those five minutes.

Looking back on my early days as a mum, I can see now how hard I was on myself. I felt like I was under so much pressure to be the perfect parent, to get everything right and have all the answers, but now I can see that the pressure only came from myself, no one else.

When I was pregnant for the first time, I thought I was ready. I had done my research into the latest gizmos for warming up bottles and safe sleep arrangements. I had rows of tiny baby grows in the drawer and books on what to do when things went wrong. I knew my life was about to change forever but I thought I was ready for it. What I wasn't at all prepared for was the irreversible change it was going to bring about in me.

I quickly learned that becoming a mother changes you. It changes the way you see the world, your priorities, your hopes and dreams, your career, and your lifestyle. It's not at all surprising that such a drastic change can also lead to a change in your mental health. I cannot speak for all mothers on this topic, only myself, but I do know that I am most definitely not alone in the way that I felt.

My transition into motherhood unfortunately was not a pleasant one. My waters broke three days before my daughter was actually born which meant I had a very long and painful dry labour. I won't bore you with all the gory details, but as I got near to her arrival, I was completely exhausted having had almost thirty hours of contractions. At this point I'd had an epidural so I could rest and have enough energy left to push when the time came. However, the effects of the epidural wore off before I actually delivered, and the midwife refused to believe that this was the case, which meant I ended up delivering with no pain relief at all.

As I held my new baby in my arms, it quickly became apparent that I had torn rather severely and required a fair number of stitches. Rather than being able to enjoy the feeling of holding my baby for the first time, I was then stitched up – without any form of pain relief as the midwife still refused to accept the fact that the epidural was no longer effective. I was sobbing and flinching the whole time, struggling to bear the pain of the stitches.

The midwife looked at me and said, 'You're a mum now, you've got to toughen up and let me do my job.'

Almost eight years later, those words still reverberate round my mind. It was as if in an instant, I no longer existed anymore in any other role than that of mum. My own feelings and fears no longer counted for anything and my sole purpose in life was to provide for my child.

Once the stitching was complete, my daughter was taken to the special baby unit to be given precautionary antibiotics due to the length of time she had been in the uterus after my waters broke. My husband went with her and I was left completely alone to try and shower. I remember standing in the wet room crying my eyes out, watching all the blood wash down the plughole, not knowing what on earth had just hit me. I was in so much pain everywhere that I couldn't even bend forward enough to pick up my underwear from the floor and get dressed again.

The next five hours were spent in a hospital room that hadn't been cleaned from the delivery. My husband and I had to sit in bloody sheets and step over the blood on the floor as I tried to adjust to my new life as a mum.

Eventually I was moved to the maternity ward where I could get some rest and sleep. Over the days that followed, family and friends came to visit us and everyone cooed over the baby, asking how I was. I vividly remember not knowing the answer to that question. I was in so much physical and emotional pain and yet still somehow numb, though I felt like everyone was expecting me to be happy because I had a beautiful baby.

Looking back, I now know that I had severe birth trauma and that my treatment at the hospital was appalling. At the time though, I was a first-time mum and had no idea that my experience was not how it should have been.

I was very angry for a long time that my birth experience had been ruined and that my first few weeks with my daughter were tainted by my trauma. The shock of the birth had stopped me from being able to bond in those early days and enjoy my baby in the way I would have liked. Thankfully there have been no lasting effects from this, and my daughter and I have always had an excellent relationship.

Consequently, when I became pregnant with a second child, I was understandably nervous about giving birth and was referred to a mental health midwife to support me through the pregnancy. Fortunately, my second birth was much less traumatic and was an all-round more pleasant experience. I gave birth to my son in a birthing pool and the care was second to none.

However, giving birth is only the beginning of the lifelong journey that motherhood takes us on, and I was soon to realise that even more challenges lay ahead.

For quite some time during my children's early years, I felt completely lost. Like I no longer knew who I was anymore, because the person I was before no longer existed. Trying to find a way to still hang on to those parts of myself that made me *me* whilst juggling the pressures of being a parent was no easy task. Finding myself thrown into this new life, where I could no longer take a pee by myself or find time to drink a hot cup of tea, took its toll on my mental state. Shortly after having my second child, I started recognising the warning signs of post-natal depression in myself and contacted my midwife.

I was very fortunate to have a supportive midwife this time around who helped me get the support I needed. My brush with post-natal depression was thankfully, a fairly mild one in comparison to a lot of women, but it did leave a lasting impression. When I look back on that period of my life, my overriding feeling was that of not being good enough and believing I was failing. A feeling I'm sure many parents have encountered at one time or another. I found the pressure of wanting to be a good mum overwhelming and almost unbearable at times. Add to that a severe lack of sleep, fluctuating hormones, and a tantrum throwing toddler, and most days I wanted to scream and cry right along with her.

As my son got older and grew into a toddler, he was a really bad sleeper. I would spend hours in his bedroom at night, waiting for him to fall asleep as he would wake frequently and struggled very much to settle by himself. This time in my life also coincided with lockdown, and the lack of interaction with other adults as well as the sleep deprivation was driving me crazy. This is when I discovered writing. I had always been an avid reader, and I decided that I would give writing a try myself. So I used to spend hours at night, typing out chapters of the very first draft of my very first book on my phone, in the dark, whilst I waited for him to fall asleep.

I quickly became hooked on my new hobby and started to take myself more seriously as an actual writer. Instead of only writing on my phone at night, I started to type my book properly and sought out some beta readers to see if I was any good. Their response to my story was overwhelming, and I was blown away by their encouragement and support. Writing made me feel better and gave me back a part of myself that I thought had been lost. Suddenly I had something that was just for me, that gave me an escape from the pressures of parenting, and made me feel good about myself again. I firmly believe that writing is what got me through lockdown and the early years of parenting and for that I will forever be grateful.

The purpose of me telling you all this is not to gain sympathy or wave my banner of bravery around. It is simply to raise awareness and to let other mothers know that it is ok to feel overwhelmed and it is ok to struggle. Finding parenting hard does not make you a bad parent. In fact, I believe quite the opposite to be true. Good parents worry so much because they care so much and are always looking for ways to be better.

However, if there's one thing I've learned, it's that in order to be a good parent, you first have to take care of yourself. Someone once said to me 'you can't pour from an empty cup' and this is so very true. If your own needs are not being met and you are not taking care of yourself, then you cannot take care of others as effectively. So my takeaway message from this – from one mother to another – would always be that you *are* good enough, and you *do* matter. Never be afraid to tell people how you are really feeling and try not to lose yourself along the way. Everyone's journey into and throughout motherhood is unique and no two people will have the exact same experiences, but it's important to remember that you are not alone, and that other people will be feeling the exact same way you are at one time or another.

My own journey as a mother is far from over, and I have no doubt that I still have many challenges and difficult times to face ahead. I still have so much to learn, I don't believe we ever really stop. However, I like to think that I am now equipped with some of the necessary tools to be able to overcome them and do the best I can for my children, which is all anyone can ever ask.

THE STRUGGLING BALLERINA

by Mia Kun

SEEING THE BEAUTIFUL BALLERINAS ON stage is an experience that stays with us forever. We look at their elegance, beauty and impossible movements. Every little girl wants to grow up to be a dancer. They all want to portray the white swan or the Sleeping Beauty. They all want to stand in their stunning costumes and dance the way the breath-taking ballerina did when they first saw her perform.

Some little girls grow up to dance, others find different passions along the way. But there are a handful of little girls who would do anything day in, day out to keep fighting for their dream, even if they were told many times that 'they don't have the right body' to succeed in this industry.

This is a story of that little girl.

I CAN'T PINPOINT the exact moment it happened, and probably there isn't just one moment. It was an accumulation of events, comments, and years of dancing in front of the mirror.

Ever since I was little, I was never content with my body. I constantly sought out different ways of losing weight or looking like everyone else in my dance class. I thought 'if I had her body, I could be as good as her'. It didn't matter how many national titles we won, or how many times I stood on stage performing, it always came back to that one single thought and feeling: the need to look slimmer.

I always loved performing, and when I was little, I looked for ways to climb on any stage and dance. It was love at first sight. Whenever I was dancing, the outside world around me quieted, and it was just me and the music. Yet I didn't start training until I was six years old, exactly two years after I wasn't accepted into the national ballet school at the age of four – as I didn't have the right body type and they thought I would grow up to struggle there. They wanted to save me from that destructive and painful path, but destiny couldn't be beaten. It wasn't really ballet that had captured my heart, it was more the junior competition team where we rehearsed the same four numbers over and over and competed with them. It was fun, the travels, the costumes, the stage, the adrenaline buzzing through our veins before the performance, and the nerve-wracking minutes before the winner was announced. We were like a family, just us ten and the teacher.

But that was the glamorous side of it, the one that would have ended up on social media, if the tool had existed back then.

What happened behind the scenes was far worse.

One particular comment stuck with me from my competitive years. I was around ten and I was getting ready to compete. At that time not everyone had their own costumes, and we would switch in between each other, sharing them. The girl, whose costume I had to take, handed me her unitard with a concerned look and asked: *'But... you won't stretch it out, right?'*

I stared at her blankly, not sure if I understood her correctly, or if she was just joking. I remember telling her something along the lines of 'no' and being mortified. It was a unitard that fit more than one size, but still something about it really bothered me. It was one thing to think and feel those things by yourself, but hearing it from others was a confirmation of everything I believed.

It shook me to the core, and her words engraved into my heart.

I was heartbroken.

And that was the beginning of everything.

AFTER THAT MOMENT, any time we had to order costumes or got our measurements taken, fear gripped my throat and paralyzed me. I hated those little numbers written next to my name with the size of my hips, legs, waist. I was no longer myself, instead I became the combination of those numbers. I was the width of my hips, the length of my legs and the square metre of my waist. Every time I would see them written down, I compared it to the others. I observed their number and wished my sizes were different, smaller, closer to the others.

Back then I didn't know much about weight.

But that was about to change soon enough.

When I turned fourteen, I wanted to audition for a performing arts high school. I got told I needed to be a certain weight to be able to audition. That summer, I was introduced to the magical number on the scale, and I tried changing up things in my diet to make sure that day by day that number decreased.

They weren't big things. I would swap my dinner for salad. Change my breakfast to fruits. Cut out carbs completely.

It was summer after all, I had an endless supply of fruits and I remember trying to eat just watermelons for days, which was basically only water and sugar.

The combination of all these things seemed to work and I reached the desired magical number on the scale and convinced my parents to let me audition.

As expected, I got accepted into their classes and come September, I was officially a student there.

That's when everything began to go downhill.

Being in such a demanding environment was different from my competitive dance classes two times a week. I went from two times a week having an hour-long class where we were going over the same choreography and barely having specific technique classes, to then moving up to three times a week for four hours a day.

But it wasn't only the hours that increased. The mentality was different too. While before we were kids from elementary school who would snack and have fun before or after our classes, the conversations took a turn in my new school. Everyone was talking about weight, sharing tips on how to lose it, telling us what they ate to stay slim or what tricks existed to lose weight quicker.

I was bombarded with all this information, my brain being overwhelmed with how important this was to every single person in my class.

It was normal for them to share and talk about it.

And it became my new normal too.

I started trying out things, like cutting out food groups, wrapping my legs in kitchen foil and using fat burning cream, making my legs burn while dancing to make sure I would sweat more. I even bought sauna suits and pants to help me sweat.

We were convinced that sweating was the key. Sweat was fat crying, after all.

Long hours in the studio meant less time to snack and eat food. We would bring healthy snacks, but usually after lunch, I started my classes and I only got home at nine, which was too late to eat dinner.

I saw the change in my body, how it grew leaner and thinner, the way I wanted it. Yet... it wasn't good enough.

There was always someone thinner than you in the class.

There was this one girl, who had severe anorexia and everyone was complimenting her on her looks, triggering her even more, while all of us wanted tricks and tips from her to find out how we could look that way.

Then another girl got called 'chubby' by our director, and a couple of months later, she was skinny and beautiful.

It became a competition to see who could develop a disorder quicker. Since my parents were quite involved, I couldn't just stop eating, they would have noticed the change, they would have picked up on it. I hid behind some diets, but the results were never as visible as for others.

I strived to hear the compliment of: *have you lost weight?* Or, *you look amazing.*

That was my main goal.

Dancing and my technique came after that.

I just wanted to hear those enchanted words and feel accomplished.

IT WASN'T UNTIL senior year when I fully tipped over. It started a year before, when my director took interest in my dancing, complimented me and allowed me to jump into even more advanced classes, instead of keeping me with my classmates. I felt proud and happy but simultaneously I wanted to prove myself.

But the only way I knew how to do that was to lose weight and fit in with all those girls, who were far more advanced and better.

I became consumed by calories. I was no longer eating a banana for breakfast, I was eating 100 calories. I was not eating a chicken breast with salad, I was consuming 400 calories. It all became about the numbers I ate. I kept a diary logging in every single thing touching my lips and counting if it fit into my 1000 calorie day.

On days when I went over it, I got upset. I've spent hours crying on the floor of my bedroom, touching my body, and wishing I could cut off the fat and mould myself in a shape that would make me happy.

Because happiness only came when I was skinny. Until then, I was destined to be miserable.

I don't remember how much time passed exactly, I just remember the day when in my high school we started the day with PE. We were skipping rope and I became lightheaded, needing to sit down. My teacher wanted to give me a sugar cube or juice to drink just to help with my blood sugar. Instead of accepting it, like any other person would, tears flooded my eyes, and I begged him not to. I didn't want anything sugary. I couldn't take anything sugary. I cried and shook my head, refusing to even look at the sugar cube in front of me.

That was the moment everyone realised something was very wrong with me.

During that week my friends all tried talking to me. They wanted to make me see that what I was doing was wrong. They tried convincing me there was nothing else I could do, my skin was already stretched over my bones, and they kept explaining to me this is how I was born. My hips were wider, they weren't as narrow and boyish as some other girls in my dance class. I was just built differently.

And I hated these excuses.

Just because I was born with a different body structure, I couldn't believe I had to suck it up and look the way I hated.

As expected, I didn't stop.

We had prom in November, where we had to wear pretty dresses. Mine looked ridiculous on me, as it was made on my old measures, and the corset was pulled in too tight to be able to hug my new body, completely ruining the dress and to this day, every time I want to show someone pictures of my prom, all I can see is how the dress is wrinkled up around my waist and it looks silly.

Christmas came after that and I spent my favourite holiday surrounded by fear, resisting eating the food we only had once a year and being excited over the fact that despite the holidays, I had managed to lose weight. Not just maintain it but lose it.

Because there wasn't a day that I didn't step on the scale.

That was the first thing I did every morning and whatever the number on the scale was it decided my mood.

If it was lower than the day before I was happy for a split second, before my brain went into obsessing over how to maintain that, what to do to make it even lower.

And if it was, God forbid, higher due to any reason, I'd spend the day miserable, on the verge of tears and annoyed.

It was a vicious cycle and I became enslaved by the numbers.

MY END-OF-YEAR BALLET exam came and it was tragic. I always excelled in ballet as it was my strongest style, but since I wanted to look confident in my leotard, I didn't eat anything before it. Throughout the whole exam I felt dizzy and lightheaded. To this date that is my worst ballet exam score and I never got a second chance to recover it. I remember despite my endless love towards ballet, I just wanted the exam to end. I was counting down the minutes until it was over. Everything was blurry, my stomach was growling and my head hurt. I hated every minute of that class.

And that wasn't me.

I loved ballet more than anything.

Soon after that I moved away to university, living alone for the first time in my life. The taste of freedom and cooking for myself. That's when the real problem started.

I never enjoyed cooking and I was terrified of gaining weight, yet...

The first thing I did was buy a scale and started eating as much as I could. There was no one watching me eat. There was no one judging. I was free to consume whatever I wanted.

I entered into a binge eating cycle of eating as much as I could because no one was there to stop me or to look after me. All the rules I'd set up for myself years ago had dissolved and I was my own biggest enemy.

I tipped to the other end and during that first year, I gained a lot of weight. No one said anything, no one commented or mentioned how fat I was, but I felt it. I could feel my skin stretching, my thighs and stomach growing from every snack I consumed. I felt my clothes fit tighter, and I saw it in my reflection. My face was growing rounder and my cheeks were becoming fuller.

After that terrible freshman year, where I gained all the weight I'd lost during my years of being careful, I entered my sophomore year with newfound motivation to get back to my old looks through a strict diet. The meal plan consisted of eating on day one: only fruits, the second day: vegetables, third day: mix of fruits and veggies, fourth day: eight bananas, fifth day: chicken and tomato, sixth day: chicken and veggies, and the seventh day, whatever I wanted.

That was the worst mix. Allowing me to binge on the seventh day, while starving all the other days.

I followed that 'meal plan' for months, until my body stopped producing enzymes necessary to digest dairy and gluten. I'd created a whole new intolerance from not eating several food groups.

That wasn't enough for me to realise I was heading down a bad path. It was fuelling me, giving me an excuse to say: *I can't eat carbs, they have gluten.* It gave me a way out of pizza nights and burgers, allowing me to pick salads whenever I had gone out with my friends.

One summer, I even decided to stay at my university town and not go home. Allowing me a summer on the beach, while I could continue down my path.

As expected from the severe restriction, my metabolism slowed down making it harder to lose weight, and I sought a new way to help my weight loss – laxatives. Taking three or four a day to keep the number on the scale decreasing. It got worse when we would go out to a restaurant with my boyfriend to eat dinner and I had to go to the bathroom right after eating to make sure I wasn't going to gain weight from the dinner. Or when we would go to the cinema and share popcorn, and I would keep taking some in my hand, so he wouldn't be suspicious, but throw it under my seat and never put a single one in my mouth.

I invented different ways to trick my body and force it to keep losing weight.

Until one day my parents noticed something was wrong and my mom flew out to come visit me, and after a long heart to heart, she took me home.

They signed me up to a ballet intensive over the summer, allowing me to take my mind off everything and enjoy dancing for the first time.

I danced during university as well, slowly re-discovering my love towards ballet, but it was more of a workout, than a passion.

For the first time that summer, I looked at it as passion.

People say you can't heal in the same environment that got you sick, but I managed to heal there.

BY THE TIME my senior year of university rolled around, I promised myself I would make the effort, start cooking and experimenting making things. I was still concerned with my looks and weight, but I was determined to do it the healthy way. Bake myself something healthy but sweet, eat whole foods and make the effort to keep a balanced life. I'd go to the gym to do cardio, followed the Beach Body workout and attended ballet classes.

It still wasn't a healthy way of life as I compensated my healthy foods with working out, but it was much better than before.

I grew to enjoy moving. I loved seeing my body get strong instead of skinny.

I was on the right path to heal, while I managed to hold onto my love for ballet.

I have never once gone to therapy, despite many people encouraging me. I found my own way of coping with things and that was writing. I started writing when I was fourteen, making up stories and writing it all down. It was an outlet to channel everything inside me, get rid of it and make me feel better.

WRITING IS OUR SUPERPOWER

Writing was the reason why I didn't need therapy. I've had my own therapy sessions every day with myself whenever it was just me and my laptop.

I write about dance. I write about eating disorders. I write about many different things, bringing awareness to people.

My stories are filled with real issues, while they are still romance.

It's my outlet to deal with uncertainty, pain and happiness. Whatever I'm feeling I pour it into my characters and stories.

Every story and every character holds a piece of me.

They all contributed to my healing. They were all by my side through my darkest periods.

They saved me, when I couldn't save myself.

EVEN THE VOID HAS SHADOWS

by M.F. Moody

I HAVE ALWAYS ADORED THE written word. From the moment I learned how to read, I've been an avid devourer of books. To not only be able to lose yourself in new worlds, but to revisit them as many times as you want? It's magical and the ultimate form of escapism. And now I have the honour of being on the other side of the page, creating entire worlds and characters for readers to enjoy. I can give them that joy out of a place of pain and darkness. I am not the first, nor will I be the last to do so. One of my favourite shows said it best: "To transform the pain of a tormented life into ecstatic beauty. Pain is easy to portray, but to use your passion and pain to portray the ecstasy and joy and magnificence of our world..." (*Vincent and The Doctor, Doctor Who).*

While 2021 saw the production of my debut novel, it was not the first time I'd seen my work published. That happened several times in my teenage years, and I still have two of the poetry anthologies that my poems were published in. They are not bright, uplifting prose full of love and sunlight—no, my poems edge toward the darker side of the emotional spectrum. You see, although I was not formally diagnosed until my mid-twenties, I have struggled with anxiety, depression, and suicidal ideologies and tendencies since my early teenage years. I am a survivor of multiple suicide attempts, self-harm, and several mental breakdowns. Writing has always been a form of catharsis for me, be it by writing poems, weaving stories, or even putting my thoughts and feelings out into the world via blog form after I moved from Australia to the United Kingdom back in late 2015.

In September of 2016, I had my second major mental breakdown. My first had occurred in my early-ish twenties, after I'd left a toxic and abusive relationship. That experience—and the resulting trauma and fallout—is best left for another time. Needless to say, it was the catalyst to my formal diagnosis.

But back to 2016. To give you an idea of what my life had been like up to that point, my family and I—consisting of my hubby, our at-the-time toddler son, and four cats—had moved from Australia over to the UK (where my hubby is from) in late 2015. While I have had experience moving—growing up with a parent in the military prepared me well—this was the first time I'd ever lived in another country and culture. And yes, while Australia and England might be close when it comes to our cultures, there are enough differences to cause issues and misunderstandings.

I'd struggled with infertility before falling pregnant with our son, and had also endured two threatened miscarriages while pregnant with him. His birth—while not as traumatic as many other women experience—was not what I would call "standard" or "smooth" as he was delivered almost two weeks early via emergency c-section. I felt overwhelmed at times, thought I was an unfit parent, and—prior to our move—had been seeing a psychiatrist for my mental health issues. I was on two different anti-depressants, and I fully credit them for being the reason I almost single-handedly packed up, sold off, and relocated an entire household's worth of furniture, a house, two cars, four cats, a dog, and a toddler within the space of four months.

My hubby flew over to the UK three months before I joined him, along with our son and four cats. The dog stayed behind with my parents, which was a devastating blow for me. The second blow came not long before my breakdown—the eldest of our cats, one I'd found abandoned and had adopted, who was the most loving, friendly, and vocally chatty cats I'd ever known—abruptly became ill. Unexpected and sudden renal failure, and there was no saving her. To this day, almost seven years on, I still miss her.

I don't remember much about my breakdown, which happened over the course of several hours. I remember sitting under the frigid waters of the shower, using a box-cutter to slice into my arms. I remember huddling over myself, manic as I picked fluff off the carpet. I remember riding in the back of an ambulance. Those memories are somewhat vague and fuzzy, but they're still there.

However, the one thing I *do* remember with pristine clarity was sometime after I'd arrived at the hospital. I was sitting in a hospital bed with my husband and three-year-old son across the room, and telling the on-call psychologist that if he gave me a loaded gun, I would blow my head off there and then, in front of my family. While it wasn't enough to get me sectioned, my downward spiral was serious enough to get me placed under the care of a mental health crisis team who would monitor me in my own home.

It worked. Somewhat.

* * *

THERE'S A SAYING, "It's always darkest before the dawn." I never really understood this, as I

have spent many a night watching the sky as it has gradually grown lighter. The stars have always been a solace for me, along with books. While not *literally* correct, you can understand and believe it to be true in a metaphorical sense.

WRITING IS OUR SUPERPOWER

When people are experiencing troubling times, it is right at their lowest point where everything seems hopeless. It is at this point where their thoughts turn bleak, they stop seeking a way out of the morass they find themselves in, and instead start to entertain thoughts of a more "final" solution. Thankfully, for most people these occasions are exceedingly rare, if not non-existent. However, there are some of us unfortunate souls who walk a path that is more often shadow than light, rocky rather than smooth, filled with pit-falls and booby-traps that would make even the most sure-footed stumble and trip up. It is we who blindly flail about in the deepening darkness, unable to even distinguish a pin-prick of light, and all too commonly give in to the blackness and give up our will to live.

Depression is often referred to as "the black dog," the faithful, unwavering companion who can sniff you out of any potential hiding spot, who will "dog" your steps, and often trip you up as it gets underfoot. I do not feel as though this moniker is justly deserved. Dogs are loyal, loving companions, whose occasional hindrance is not done out of malicious intent, but rather a desire to stay close to you. No, I picture depression more as a violent storm at sea, a combination of tempest and maelstrom, unforgiving both overhead and beneath you. I once wrote the following when I was struggling, and I think it sums up just how powerful and even seductive such emotional upheaval can be:

"Screams dart and tumble around inside your head like bats on wing at night, feasting on despair and self-recriminations. You fight against them, using the light provided by love and happier memories, but they are too quick, twisting away, escaping only to come back again to attack you when you are unprepared. Your heart races, your stomach churns as fear turns to blind panic. You try to breathe, but are

suffocated under the weight of the darkness. You struggle to find any handhold, to pull yourself out from under the crashing waves, but they pummel you down further into blackness. You flail about, surfacing briefly, before being dragged down by the weight of your fears. You feel your lungs burn as they try to drag in air, you struggle to find safe harbour. Miraculously, you find a rocky spur to cling to, your head barely above the crashing, sucking waves. You have been given a brief respite, but for how long?"

There have been several times in the past where I have found myself at a point where I could only see darkness. Not the dark of an overcast night on a new moon, nor the blackness of a light-proof room you step into after being in bright sunlight. Not even the pitch-black you might find in caves deep under the earth. No, this was a darkness so deep, the abyss itself had deep shadows, and even those voids had shadows of their own. These varying levels of blackness would entice me inside, and the deeper the shade, the more seductive the urge to implement that "final solution." It was only through sheer force of will—and the remembrance of promises I've made to my mother, husband, and son—that stayed my hand. They are three of the "rocky spurs" to which I cling with a desperation to stay this side of that razor's edge between life and oblivion. Writing is one of the others. It is both a catharsis and a salvation, enabling me to purge my darkest thoughts without further harming myself. The road ahead is long and difficult, but with some amazing friends, and wonderful family, I will get there.

It is very easy for people who have never experienced mental illness to either dismiss it, or to deride people who have taken their own lives as "weak" and "selfish." In actual fact, most people who take their own lives—and I'm not talking about murder-suicides, that's a different kettle of fish—do so in the belief that they are actually helping their loved ones, taking the burden that they see themselves as being from the shoulders of family and friends, knowing that because "life goes on," their families would eventually move on with their lives and do so without the burden of their illness weighing them down.

It is equally hard for people who have never experienced mental illness to understand how a person is feeling, as even those who may suffer from the same illness will have different triggers and coping mechanisms. So while they may understand what a person is going through, they cannot understand how you feel because their experiences are different. The best thing anyone can offer, rather than sympathy or empathy, is the genuine offer of company and friendship, or even a quiet place to sit, with no expectations of interaction and no demands for attention.

* * *

IN THE YEARS since my last breakdown, I have edged dangerously close to that precipice on more than one occasion. This is despite (or perhaps due to) all of the changes made with my medication. I was taken off one, had another's dosage maxed-out, then had to switch to yet another when the maxed-out one stopped working. That was before I was taken off *all* my meds in early 2020 because my GP wanted to "reset" my brain because they were no longer working for me. Yes, you read that right. Early 2020. I have gone through the entire shit-show that was the global pandemic completely unmedicated. I do *not* recommend that experience.

Luckily for me, I have a very supportive husband. He encouraged me to start writing again. He paid for me to get my first manuscript edited, and also paid for the image I used for the cover. While the story itself may not be about issues around mental health, it was the product of my own battle against my inner darkness. It gave me something to focus on, an outlet for my fears, my frustrations, and my unspoken hopes and dreams. It's not the most awe-inspiring piece of literature, but it's real, and it's mine, and it was the gateway into a world I once could only imagine being a part of.

My struggle with the highs and lows of my mental health journey is ongoing. As someone who has been clinically diagnosed with anxiety, moderate-to-severe recurrent depressive disorder (I believe this incorporates both major depressive disorder and persistent depressive disorder), and seasonal affective disorder, I don't believe I'll ever escape from the nightmarish cycle. The wonderful thing, though, is that I have a fantastic network of people who are willing to lift me up when I stumble and carry me through some of my darkest times. Some of these are my family. Others are lifelong friends. And then there are my fellow authors, who have welcomed me with open arms and do their best to love and support me through each episode.

I don't know if reading my experiences has helped you in any way or given you any insight into what it's like to live with depression and anxiety. For those who have experienced a similar battle, take solace. We are here, hands outstretched to help and guide you.

You are not alone.

MY DARK SHADOW

by Marie Anne Cope

THAT'S WHAT I CALL MY depression. Like a shadow, depression is always with me but not always visible. There is no cure for it, or other mental illnesses, for that matter; there are only plasters to cover the gaping chasm. Over the years I've learned to recognise when I'm teetering on the edge of the abyss, I've learned to accept the shadow that dogs me wherever I go, but most of all, I've learned that I am not broken. I don't need fixing. I just need understanding.

"Hello darkness, my old friend. I've come to talk with you again..."
(The Sound of Silence, Simon & Garfunkel)

I'm writing this now while my dark friend looks over my shoulder. Over the past three months, I've had an operation on my leg, I've been plagued with shingles, my family have had to make the awful decision to put my dad in a residential home and I have been a shoulder for my mum to cry on. Throughout this, I have continued to run my business; I have continued to developmentally edit novels, and I have continued to move my various writing projects forward. None of these caused my sinister friend to put in an appearance.

What tipped me over the edge and had me opening the door and inviting the darkness in was feedback on the first chapter of a novel I was on the verge of launching. The novel is in a new genre (women's fiction) and I penned it during lockdown. It is the happiest I have ever been writing anything and my gut told me, "This is the one." This is the book to catapult my writing into the stratosphere, so to speak. I invested in a Curtis Brown novel writing course, which included a critique of my first three chapters. I was a little puzzled when the feedback said it reminded her of Liane Moriarty's *Big Little Lies*, as that is a psychological thriller and mine is women's fiction. But I didn't question it as this was a Writing a Romance Novel course, so I presumed I'd missed something in both the TV series and the book.

I polished my novel following the course and pitched it to agents with no success. When I went on a writing retreat last year, I was advised to forget the agent, as all they do is take your money, and send it directly to publishers. And so, I did, with the same result, although one said my novel had a great premise.

In March I went on another writing retreat run by the same best-selling women's fiction author, and I told her about my lack of progress. She agreed to review my first chapter to see if she could help. The look on her face after she'd read it told me all I needed to know. She said she was waiting for the murderer to jump out all the while she was reading. When I asked why, she said because of the dark language style, it reads like a psychological thriller, not a women's fiction novel.

Whilst a light bulb flicked on regarding the response I had on the Curtis Brown course, my confidence and belief in my ability to write shattered, with each shard reflecting the shadow looming over me. Even her telling me I have a great story, I just need to change the way I tell it, didn't help.

I know one hundred per cent she is right, but that doesn't help at this stage. That is what pushed me over the edge, and all I can do now is take the steps necessary to pick myself up, dust myself down and pick up my pen again. And I will... eventually.

"Can you hear me now? I'm not doing fine. I'm drowning in my mind again."
(High Enough, Lisa Marie Presley)

Those who don't suffer from depression don't understand what it's like. Because—like all mental illness—it's invisible, they think comments like: "Pull yourself together" or "You'll be fine after a good night's sleep," will somehow magically make it all go away. It won't.

My dark shadow will never go away but when it looms too large, as it does every so often, I make an appointment to speak to my therapist, I write down what I am feeling, and sometimes, like now, I even share it with others in the hope that by putting my situation out into the world, I might help someone else in some small way. But most of all, I tell myself it's okay to feel the way I do, and I take time to be kind to myself because I know, one day soon, the clouds will retreat for a while.

"It's not easy facing up when your whole world is black."

(Paint it Black, The Rolling Stones)

It's taken me a long time to recognise when I'm opening myself up to the darkness, but now that I can, I am able to tread water until I am strong enough to turn my face to the sun once more.

To show you how my old friend likes to show up, here are a couple of diary entries I adapted into blog posts:

13 Oct 2019: But I Thought You Were Happy...

FOR WEEKS NOW, the Dark Shadow has been stalking me, reaching its tendrils out to latch onto me and drag me ever closer to the edge. I've resisted, as I always do, but for the first time in a very long time, I have stared over the edge, into the abyss. Last night, in fact, I leaned over.

Sitting in the bath, *Bat Out of Hell II* playing in the background, tears coursing down my cheeks, the voices urging me on; I stared into the water, my face millimetres from the surface, and I wanted desperately to know what it would feel like to inhale that lavender-scented water into my lungs. Would it be painful, as they say? Would my body reject it, or would it do as it was told and yield? To quieten the voices, to calm the storm, to close the doors on the world – this is what the Dark Shadow was offering me.

But as my nose disappeared beneath the surface, a tiny voice whispered, "Help me." This voice grew stronger and stronger until I realised it wasn't inside my head. I was speaking. I was uttering those two life-altering words out loud. I was finally asking the universe for help. I was acknowledging I couldn't defeat the Dark Shadow alone.

I don't know why the Dark Shadow comes, but I have, over the years, learned to recognise its presence. It's a weight in my chest, a veil over my eyes, a cloud blocking my thoughts. But, more than anything, it's the voices in my head; not the ones who craft my stories, but the ones who want to remind me of my station – you're not good enough, your writing is crap, you have no talent, you're getting old, you're ugly, you've got no boobs, you'll get fat if you eat that, no one loves you, no one will miss you, what's the point in you. These were the voices forcing my face under the water. These were the voices who nearly won this time, but for that one voice that spoke out—that inner strength of which I am most proud—and asked for help.

I don't remember how long it took following my plea, but I know that before I went to bed, I felt a little lighter, and when I woke up this morning, I saw a sliver of light through the darkness.

What pulled me back from the edge? Did the universe intervene, and my guides stop me? Did my willpower suddenly cause me to dig in my heels to prevent my fall? Or was it a combination of both? Whatever, or whoever, it was, I am grateful.

I believe it is some traits that are good about me that make me vulnerable to the Dark Shadow. My compassion, my empathy, and my vivid imagination all contribute to my greatest weakness. The state of the world right now – climate change, wildfires, animals in peril, the farce that is Brexit, the hatred, disrespect and vileness of humanity – has all been too much. And, once the chink in my armour is exposed, the voices begin.

The voices come from inside, fed and nurtured by my interactions with the world, filtered through my fragile confidence, to become something more than they initially were.

Listening as I am told I should wear makeup and dress up more, that a real writer writes every day and sells thousands of books, that I should write romance or erotic fiction not "that rubbish you write" – that I shouldn't watch the films and shows I do, that I should socialise more, that I shouldn't fall in love so easily, that I shouldn't pin my future on a pipe dream, that I shouldn't be interested in the stuff I am as it means I'm not right in the head.

Hearing that I am not good enough, that I am not pretty enough, that no one will love me, that I'm not worth being with, that I am a failure, that my writing is rubbish and I am wasting my time, that my creativity is a joke, that my dreams are a delusion, that no one will want someone like me, that I am broken.

Listening vs hearing is a daily battle. Most of the time, I can block out the voices, but sometimes they take over, and occasionally, like last night, they almost win.

7 Aug 2019: Learning to Love Myself...

I FOUND OUT today that, despite all the work I keep doing, and despite what I keep telling myself, I don't love myself. How do I know this? A good friend pointed it out to me.

For a change, it wasn't about my disastrous relationships, despite another having just hit the dust. We were just having a general chat over dinner before heading to a concert. So, when she said, "You don't love yourself," my hackles went up, and I immediately went on the defensive:

"Yes, I do... or I think I do."

"No, you don't," she persisted, offering nothing further.

I continued to munch on my sweet potato fries before venturing the question I wasn't entirely sure I wanted an answer to: "What makes you say that?"

"You put yourself down all the time."

"I do not," came back my immediate response.

"Yes, you do."

"When? Give me an example."

"Just before, when we were talking about your website."

I frowned as I looked at her. I had no idea what she was talking about.

"When you were saying you couldn't change the sign-up form on your home page."

"That's not putting myself down. That's stating a fact."

"No, it isn't. It's putting yourself down. If you loved yourself, you would have said you hadn't *yet* figured out how to change the sign-up form."

It's weird, but until she pointed it out, I had never viewed comments such as "can't" as a putdown, but the more I think about it, the more I can see her point.

To truly love myself, I must believe in myself completely, knowing deep down I can do, or find a way to do, pretty much anything.

I was a bit flummoxed because I honestly thought I loved myself. Now, I'm back to asking where this tendency not to love myself comes from?

A couple of years ago, after another failed relationship, I decided I was done, that I was going to focus solely on me and do everything to please me. It worked. I was happy. I loved my life. I was confident, healthy, had a great social life, and I loved me, or so I thought.

Then I was "persuaded" to date someone who had yet to get divorced. Everything was going great. We talked, laughed, holidayed, made plans for the future, and believed we were soulmates. Then the divorce proceedings started, and it all went sour, to the point we broke up. His doing, not mine.

Despite my common sense telling me it was timing and circumstances, the little voice, the one I thought I'd finally silenced in my year of abstinence, piped up again, telling me I was innately unlovable.

So, again I ask, where does it come from? Why do I believe I am unlovable?

When I was a teenager, I fell in with the wrong crowd. My best friend and I liked to pretend we were older than our fourteen years and frequented the local pubs. Here we met a group of older guys, and it wasn't long before romances blossomed. It never occurred to me anything bad would happen. I believed I could take care of myself. After all, I'd refused to take the drugs they liked to inject regularly.

But nothing prepared me for what happened. After all, why would this man hurt me when he professed to love me? But hurt me, he did. He stripped me of my innocence, without my consent, and didn't want anything to do with me afterwards.

I blamed myself. For years I kept it inside, never telling a soul what had happened, berating myself for putting myself in that position, for believing his words, for not fighting back. It was only through therapy – a place I have been multiple times over the years – I finally understood what had happened to me, and that I was not to blame, nor was it a reflection on me. Whilst finally I accepted the first two points, the last point, despite me believing otherwise, I clearly haven't accepted.

If I believed it wasn't a reflection on me, then why, each time I have sex, do all the insecurities come crashing back in? Why then, each time I'm told I am loved, do I question it?

Over the years, broken relationships have sent me back to therapy, searching for answers to the question of, "What is wrong with me?" – refusing to accept there is nothing.

My therapist made a breakthrough when he said I look for people who are broken and then fix them. The trouble is, I only end up fixing them for the next person, because I throw in the towel long before then. He said it wasn't my job to fix people.

This reminds me of a recent session with my nutritionist, who is also a healer. I was spilling my guts, as I tend to do, and she asked, "Yes, but who fixes you?" My only reply was, "I wasn't aware I was broken." Even as I said it, I knew it was a lie. I went on to tell her about my ability to detach my spirit from my body when I encounter unwanted attention. This scares me on so many levels, and I trace it back to the loss of my innocence all those years ago—it being my brain's way of protecting me from what was happening to my body.

As I told her all this, she kept asking, "In how many previous lives were you a sex therapist?" I kept shaking my head and carried on talking, but she repeated the question, over and over, until a number popped into my head.

"Seven," I said and fell silent, the weight finally lifting from my shoulders as realisation dawned. Her simple question made complete sense to me, although, as she pointed out, I am not a sex therapist in this life.

It's clear my journey to self-love is far from over, and I do not know how long it will take. Maybe it's an endless journey. If so, I best start enjoying the ride a bit more!

THE PAST AND I

by Anonymous

Trigger Warning - Mentions of CA, SA, DV, BULLYING, SH & More. Read with caution, please.

"I'll always be a work in progress, and that's ok. The best stories haven't been written yet and when they are, the plot twists will always be the ones we remember." Me, age 36.

WRITING IS MY SUPERPOWER. BUT so is living.

I was born in the mid-Eighties and we didn't really understand what mental health was then, let alone how to overcome the things that happened to us. Our parents never spoke of feelings, their pasts kept repeating and they didn't know how to deal with it, so they didn't. Trauma was swept under the carpet and no one spoke of the family's secrets. The family shame.

We were left to deal with things ourselves, and it created a generation striving for change.

Living mostly unsupervised, children of that time had freedom beyond what we should have had. But so did those older than us. And the things that went on behind closed doors stayed behind closed doors. Unspoken. Without consequence.

Early Years

MY MOTHER HAD four children before she had my older brother. She lived a hard life with two ex-husbands who didn't offer to help. She worked two jobs and lived in garages, tiny flats, and sometimes on people's couches. Her youngest was a teenager when she met my dad. They got married quickly while she was pregnant with my brother. By the time I was born, though, she was pretty much done raising children. I'm not saying she didn't provide what we needed. We had what we needed: food, clothes and toys. We went on family holidays to campsites and made memories at the beach. But they did not supervise us much. I spent a lot of time alone or playing with neighbours at the end of the street. I had rules, and I followed them for fear they would smack my butt. But all in all, those first four, maybe five years, were good. I had my tonsils out and glasses made. I could see and breathe. But the happy childhood I had was about to end.

The details remain in my mind, never to be fully explained. But one of my mum's other sons sexually abused me. And it changed my whole being.

Mum turned to alcohol and food to cope with her own traumatic past. Taken into care at a young age, she never adjusted to living with her father and evil stepmother later on. She made mistakes. But when she met my dad, she was given the normalcy and stability she had always craved. Devoted to a fault, my dad helped care for us kids, but his first priority was always his wife. His parents were somewhat involved with us as we grew up, but an event would see us move to the coast, a two-hour journey away, so we became isolated from our extended family.

This event didn't involve me, but my six-year-old brain didn't know that.

I remember the first time I told someone I was being abused. It was the night of the event I won't detail, but as I sat in the back of my grandad's car, my dad crying in the front seat, I blurted my secret.

"Is it because *name we don't speak* does bad things to me?"

You see, my abuser made sure I believed my family would break apart if they found out. That it would be my fault and Mummy would be ever so upset with me. Snippets I managed to get throughout the night as the event happened confirmed my family was indeed breaking apart. They were upset. My dad was so angry and my mum was at home, alone.

Name we do not speak had done something bad and everyone had found out. That's all I knew.

Had they found out what he was doing to me?

I'll never forget the next thing that was said.

"Not now, *my name*! There are more important things going on. Shut up." His angry tone shut me right up. My lips clamped together and, for the longest time, they didn't utter a word of my abuse.

My parents got over the event, and we moved away from the problem. All was well, wasn't it? I was free from the abuse.

We lived in a caravan for a while, then a smelly flat above some shops and cooked toast on an upturned gas heater. We visited a place I thought might be a police station and again I tried to speak up.

"Are we getting *name we don't speak* arrested?"

I got no answer. Just exhausted sighs and lack of eye contact.

Name we don't speak didn't get arrested. Ever. He didn't have to face the consequences of his actions.

But I did.

Many years later, I would ask my mum about my childhood. She told me I would get sore often, and she would put cream on me to help. But despite her being abused as a child, she never saw the signs I was being abused.

A few times when she was drunk, which was every night, she would tell me she knew something was happening to me, but she didn't know who was doing it. I think she thought it was my dad. She asked me a few times if anything bad was happening to me, and I would say no, remembering what *name we do not speak* had told me. She could have pushed harder, she could have asked who it was, but she didn't. And when I told her who it was, she did nothing. She should have.

But she made sure I knew the name and details of the man who abused her as a child. He was her reason for drinking, for not protecting me, for everything. And I had to listen to her over and over, tell me how it affected her. Over the years, I tried to talk to her about my abuse, but I stopped when I started to believe her experience was more important than mine. That my abuse didn't matter. Hers did.

When I got older and had put in the years of work to live with my past, I asked my parents why nothing was done about my abuse.

"We didn't know whether to believe you." My dad's words have stuck with me to this day. My mother remained silent.

She has dementia now. My window for answers, for an apology, is over. My dad remains her devoted husband and I help take care of her and him. Despite everything, or maybe because of. Because I want to be better.

But...

What happened to me was buried deep. So deep.

My family was never the same after that. My parents argued all the time. Screaming matches, I couldn't help but try to break up. I knew why they argued; it wasn't because of me or what happened to me. But I still felt guilty. That would continue until I was well into my teens.

My first period came as a surprise. I didn't know why I was bleeding or how, but I hid it, thinking it would go away. Mum found my hidden underwear. She was so angry at me, and my next memory is just accepting I bled once a month and that was that. It was a dirty thing I should hide from everyone. I wasn't to speak of it and no one explained what it meant.

My mind was over-sexualized, perhaps because of the abuse, and I soon discovered adult things. By the time I was thirteen, I'd had multiple boyfriends and thought little of it. We didn't do IT, just kiss, but it felt as though I was grown. I wasn't allowed to wear the clothes I wanted. I had to cover up. Not show too much flesh. I couldn't dance the way my body wanted to.

Goth music became everything to me. All things dark and odd. It was through my love of odd things that I discovered self-harm. I don't recall a lot of my childhood, or what triggered the memories, but I do remember the first time I ever cut myself.

After an argument with my mum, a regular thing for us, I decided, rather oddly, to unfurl a metal coat hanger and bar my bedroom door with it. Why? I don't recall. I wanted to be alone, I guess. There was no lock on my door and the hanger would tell them to leave me alone. So I thought.

Sometime later, my mum pushed her way into my room and demanded to know why I had barred the door. My dad followed and together they pushed and pushed until I came up with something other than the actual reason. Because I couldn't tell them I was hurting inside. I couldn't bring up the past. I wasn't allowed to.

"I found a knife in my toy box and was going to cut myself!"

Mum's face relaxed, and they stopped shouting.

They'll tell me it's ok, that I don't have to do that. They love me and will see that I'm in pain. They can help me.

Right?

"Don't block your door again." My mum turned on her heel and left. Dad right behind her.

I knew what my mum was waiting to hear. She thought I would say my dad was abusing me and that's why I blocked my door. That's why I was acting so strangely. That's what was wrong with me.

He wasn't. Never did. Never would.

I stood in that small room, staring at my toy box for the longest time. I didn't have a knife, but I did have a shard of glass under my bed from an old, broken picture frame.

They don't care if I cut myself. If I bleed out the pain I have inside.

So why not do it?

What would follow would develop into a lifelong affliction. Twenty-three years later and I still fight that demon around my neck, the one that begs me to bleed.

Teenage

THROUGHOUT MY TEENAGE years, alongside self-harm of the slicing variety, I began to overeat. Sneaking food and sweets whenever I had the chance. I quickly gained weight and became the victim once more, bullied mercilessly because of how I looked.

By the time I left high school, I wore a size 22. I still have my prom outfit. Red trousers, because "fatties shouldn't wear dresses," my mind told me, and a red sparkly top. I loved it. But I couldn't show my arms. They were bigger than the other girl's legs. I know because they would measure during PE. My mum got me a white jacket to wear over the top. I looked very much like a middle-aged woman who worked 9-5 in an office, not a fifteen-year-old girl at her prom.

We couldn't afford a limo, and my friends had fallen out with me, as they often did, so I went with two people no one else wanted to go with. I remember seeing all the other girls with their beautiful dresses and fancy hair. I French plaited my hair and did my own make-up with cheap stuff bought from the supermarket. But I wasn't beautiful. So it didn't matter.

I left school with no friends, though you would think leaving school and starting college would give me a fresh start. But it didn't. Anxiety riddled, unable to make friends, I spent the first six months alone. I ostracised myself before the other students could. I didn't need friends and any friends I did eventually make weren't true friendships.

The first time I went to an adult night club, I was fourteen. By the time I started art college, I was a pro. My favourite outfit was a black, long-sleeved jumper and my old school pants. I was fat and ugly, and no one would be interested in me, so I didn't need to dress up. Even if I wanted to, I couldn't. There were no shops that made sexy going-out outfits for girls my size.

Then I met J.

J was older than me. Four, maybe five years, I don't recall. I was sixteen when we met and halfway through my first year in art school. I had seen him before at a friend's house. The first time I met him, J had a girlfriend. A plus-size girl like me. I remember the jealousy burning me like lava as I watched her sit in his lap and giggle.

Later, a rare night out with my friend A and her boyfriend would see the beginning of the next chapter in my life. J was single... and he wanted to kiss me. I had to remove my black lipstick, but it was worth it for a kiss. So I thought. I remember on the way to the new club I fell over because I wore wedges. I should have taken that as a sign. My guardian angel was telling me to turn back and go home.

But I didn't.

We quickly became a couple. We met the next day and then spent the first six months in heaven. It was everything my young mind thought was the ideal relationship. He took my virginity and then my dignity. We spent every spare moment together in the woods behind my house. And then my bedroom.

"Don't sign up for next year. Get a job so we can save for a house together."

Those words were a promise that turned into hell. And I did nothing to stop it. And no one noticed it was happening.

Again.

Slowly, J would turn me into a shell of a person. I accepted his comments. His fists. His kicks. His rape. I worked, cooked, cleaned, and nothing else. I had no personality, no thoughts of my own. J drank every night, like my mum, so I paid the bills and rent. I watched him drink himself stupid every night. It was my fault he drank because I made him so angry. I never knew what I did, but it must be true since he was beating me and then would rape me.

I thank the lucky stars that at that time, in that situation, I didn't get pregnant.

I didn't tell because what good would telling do? I never let them see. Clothes hid the marks and a well-practiced mask hid the pain. A mask I wore well. A mask I had been wearing since I was a child. The one that slipped later on but I now wear it again.

It seemed I was destined to be a victim. My first proper boyfriend was a monster. My friends saw but did nothing, and if my family knew, they never said or did anything. Maybe I deserved it for telling? Maybe I just deserved it. Full stop. The end. This was my life. I had to accept it.

And I did for almost three years.

The last time he hurt me, I managed to call the police. But that didn't turn out too well.

Holding my hand, he greeted the police at our door and welcomed them into our trashed underground flat. It was soon after this that my mind broke.

He was told to not have any contact with me for three months. Despite it all, this broke me. Alone in the home I worked so hard for, I'm ashamed to admit I lost my mind. I called his mother constantly, a woman who wouldn't allow me in her house because I was fat. "Why can't you get a normal girlfriend? Why get with a fatty?" she once asked him in front of me. His response was to laugh and agree. It was what it was. I was fat, I couldn't disagree.

The strain saw me get fired from a job I loved in the care industry. I lost my first home.

Shortly after that, my parents sent me to stay with my grandparents because they didn't know how to handle me. My grandad paid for a cover-up tattoo of J's name on my arm and then sent me back to my parents because I broke a rule of their house.

I was alone again. I turned eighteen.

But that wasn't the last time I saw J.

Before meeting me, he had a girlfriend his own age. He got her pregnant. But she left him, had the baby and he never heard from her. Shortly after moving back home, when the police arrested him, he got back with his ex. But that didn't stop him from begging to meet me.

So, we spent the next five months fucking in every public place we could find. We didn't get caught, but I don't know how. I knew he was with his ex, but it was almost as if I couldn't let him go.

I was caught in a trauma bond.

During this time, he didn't abuse me in any way, but he would tell me about his girlfriend and their child. I was so mentally checked out that I kept seeing him every night. I thought he would change and come back to me. But I soon realized I couldn't go back to him.

Adult Years

BEFORE I TURNED nineteen, I met my now husband.

The beginning of happily ever after.

K came into my life most surprisingly.

He lived 100 miles away, was three years older than me, and had charm as long as the day was long. Funny, adorable, and loving, I found my prince charming by randomly texting a dating app while working in a nursing home in the middle of the night.

I'd love to tell you it was every girl's dream from day one and that we have lived the dream since. But it would be a lie.

The thing with trauma is that it doesn't magically disappear when you're safe. When you're loved and free. But the reality is that trauma has a way of destroying that safety, that love, that freedom.

I was still very much actively self-harming when I met K. It had become a part of me. Part of my very being. And poor K didn't know how much worse it would become.

Our love was born from trauma. His ex abused and cheated on him, and you know some of what my ex did to me. To say we were traumatized young adults just doesn't cover what we were.

And so our whirlwind romance was just that; a whirlwind. We weren't good to each other in those first years. Neither of us knew what a healthy relationship was or how to heal ourselves. His parents didn't provide him with a blueprint of what love should be, since their marriage was more of a case of convenience than love. And my past meant I had no idea how to even live, let alone love someone.

But love him I did.

Then I got pregnant.

I remember being eleven and pretending to have a baby bump, walking around with a friend who did the same. Feeling like I was the most special person in the world. I knew I wanted children even then. I would call myself a mummy without children. So when I fell pregnant with K, it seemed as though finally, finally, I was going to get everything I had always wanted. I would have the family I craved and my life would be perfect from that point on. We were excited, but K's parents were not.

"What the fuck do you think you're playing at?" his dad yelled when K told him the news.

That's ok. We don't need them. My parents were over the moon I was pregnant. And I wasted no time texting all my family members that I was pregnant.

I started bleeding and my dreams melted into a pile of ash.

We lost our baby. And we wouldn't get the chance to be parents for another eight years. And those years were hard.

The loss didn't really hit me until my due date came and I spiralled into a deep depression.

K was the only person to show me compassion for my self-harm and it became normal that when we argued, I harmed myself. I didn't see it at the time, but I used it as a way to get his affection, his care, and his love. That's disgusting, isn't it? I know. And I'll never make up for all that I put him through. But I'll try until the day I die.

WE TRIED TO get pregnant for eight very long, very dark years. After all I had already been through, you'd think infertility wouldn't hurt me the most, but it did.

You see, I learned that if I could control everything, then I could live with my past, not forget, not heal from it, but I could live. I taught myself how to face paint and make balloon animals and did that for a time. Then I taught myself how to groom dogs. I loved animals and began to adopt them when they needed me most.

We adopted an elderly dog called Princess who was in dire need of love and care.

I slept all day and was awake all night. I didn't take care of myself and put on more and more weight. Despite K loving me the way he did, I had never felt more useless.

I couldn't do the one thing women are meant to do and have a baby.

We got married on our fifth anniversary. A simple, budget affair I'm proud and happy to say has stuck. We've been together for seventeen years this year.

I started to read about true lives. Cathy Glass books became my therapy. I read about other people being abused and coming through the other side and felt better about my past. Because if they could suffer such awful things, worse than what I had gone through, then so could I. Right?

The first clue I had that I was pregnant was when I was helping a fellow groomer because she was pregnant and couldn't lift the dogs into the bath. Her mum offered me a cup of tea at the end of a hard day, and I cried like a baby. A few weeks later, I lay on the sofa and squished my boob, crying out in pain.

At this point I had completely given up. I was a waste of breath. I couldn't have a family.

But I peed on the stick, popped it back in the box, gave it to my husband and went downstairs to let the dogs out. I didn't want to see that one red line.

I'll never forget K's face when I walked back into the living room. His smile spread from one ear to the other.

He lifted the test for me to see.

Two red lines.

Two.

"Oh, shit." That's all we could say for at least forty minutes after.

I'm pregnant. Really pregnant.

Oh, shit.

Over the next eight months, I took a total of thirty-two tests just to make sure, even when we had our first scan. I had my very first panic attack on the way into the hospital room for our eight-week scan. My parents came to them all, and there were lots of them. They travelled for three hours just to be there. I had many panic attacks and hospital visits during my pregnancy. Of course, the universe cursed me with an anterior placenta, where it sits between the baby and my stomach so I couldn't feel a lot of the movements, and that made me spiral at least three times a week.

I couldn't possibly be blessed with a child after everything, could I?

In 2014, O was born.

Healthy, tiny, and perfect, our son changed our entire lives.

All my worries were over... Right?

That's when anxiety made itself a home inside my mind.

I checked on him every hour for the first six months. Every day. Every night. I had to know he was breathing. That he was ok. That I wasn't in a straitjacket in a mental hospital, having lost my ever-loving mind.

A thought I sometimes still get today. Amongst others.

He's eight now. Has my attitude and it drives me potty, but he's honestly the best kid I've ever known. No, really. He's kind, sweet and helpful. And he's had the childhood I should have had. Protected, loved, spoiled (a little too much, but shh). He skipped all the "terrible" stages and seems to instinctively know when I need "mummy time", which means I get cuddles, a movie, and chocolate. Sometimes I need silence. Sometimes I need to hold his hand while he watches TV, or I need to take extra-long showers so I can cry without him seeing it.

I STILL STRUGGLE. The ending, or rather, the current point in my journey, isn't all butterflies and lollipops. I won't lie to you.

Every day is still a struggle. And sometimes I'm ashamed to admit that. I have a loving husband. We have our issues and my mind likes to make things up, but we have an amazing son. We have a nice house and a sustainable income. I should be in my happy place and I want to be. But that's not how this works.

Shortly after O was born, I was diagnosed with fibromyalgia, an incurable chronic pain condition that doesn't really respond to pain meds or anti-depressants. I've had arthritis since I was a girl, which mainly affects my knees and spine. I'm pre-diabetic and have asthma. Leaving my house requires days' notice and meds. I can't work normal jobs because of my health, that's why I wish I'd worked more when I was younger. I suffer with unwelcome thoughts. Flashes, I call them. Images and videos in full HD of me harming myself in too-graphic ways. And most often, I get an utter feeling of not wanting to wake up in the morning. Of utter despair. Though I have only self-harmed twice in the last eight years, so there's progress there. I'd like it to be zero, but I'll always be a work in progress. And that's ok.

O IS EIGHT now, but we've had no more pregnancies. And it looks like we won't.

I'm not ok with this, but it is what it is.

Many times in my life, I have wished I were no longer here. I truly think I should have gone to therapy. Should have checked into a facility once or five times. So...

Why didn't I?

The first time I reached out to a doctor about my mental state, they had me take a test on his computer. Bear in mind, I was in my twenties and was still self-harming.

"No one has scored that high." He informed me, his face pale and eyes wide.

What came next? "Book another appointment. We've run out of time."

I didn't book another appointment. So, what did I do?

I talked to my husband. But he couldn't listen to it all.

That was when I decided the only person who could help me live, was me.

I started to sleep at night and be awake during the day. I ate right but oddly didn't lose weight. K did, though, because of course he could lose it easily. I have endometriosis and polycystic ovaries. Yay for me.

But what really saved me, who really saved me, was O.

I knew I had to work on myself for him. I'm not suggesting you should have a child just to work on yourself. Please don't think having a kid works like that. But it worked for me. I knew I wanted to do everything I could to NOT be my parents. To not let my son have childhood trauma and I didn't want him to share mine like I did my mother's. O will never know what happened in my past, that's not his burden to carry.

I began to read. I read everything I could get my hands on before finally choosing romance as my go-to. I didn't want realistic lives; I wanted adventure. So PNR became my favourite. I lived a thousand lives before I created my own stories. Writing became everything and it still is.

But it's scary writing about my own life. In my books, I'm always the lead character. I give myself the body I've always wanted, the powers, the love(s) of their lives, and I take them on adventures beyond what is actually possible. I write their history like I'm rewriting my own. I give them trauma, but I give them the power to not only overcome, but thrive. And in turn, I gave myself the power to live with my past. I forgive myself. None of it was my fault, but it is my responsibility to make sure those I love never have to know the dark world I've known.

Despite everything, I love my parents and care for both of them. I'm not overly close to my brother, but I adore his kids. I tell people I love them every chance I get.

Working on myself, loving myself, that's harder. I still don't have friends. I tend to give too much of myself and end up hurt. I keep to myself. It's lonely and isolated, but that's just the way things go.

Self-care comes in many forms. Reading. Showering. Just brushing your teeth is an act of immense self-care.

The girl who was abused and bullied isn't the woman talking to you now, but every time I straighten my hair, brush my teeth, apply moisturizer or cleanse my face, read a good book... that little girl smiles. And I smile back at her. I became the mum I wished I had as a kid, the one I should have had. O will never question if I love him or not.

Living with trauma is the hardest thing in the world to do. Ending your life might seem the answer, but that just passes the pain to those who love you. I can't do that to O no matter how dark the days get. So I live.

"We can be the end to the cycle. But we'll have to suffer to get there."
Me, age 36

I AM YOU, YOU ARE ME, WE ARE TOGETHER!

by Steve Moore

Hi there. My name's Steven and I'm an alc...

I FIRST OPENED UP ABOUT my mental health struggles to my brilliant wife when they re-emerged to kick me in the teeth nine or so years ago, which was when I initially began to understand them myself for the first time. I had suffered with those struggles since way before Leslie and I met in early 2011, but I had been in a good place for a few years and hadn't ever felt the need to share them with her. Why would I burden someone else with that for no reason, right?

It was another few years later that I decided to go public with it, again, for the first time. In truth, this was mainly for selfish reasons, as it made me a little more comfortable if I met friends or people at author events knowing they might already have some kind of an idea about "my issues", as I called them. Yet, after I received so many kind messages from those who had read my posts on various Facebook forums — my personal page, my own author groups, and other authorly groups I was a member of — telling me how my words and my honesty had helped them too, and thanking me for my "bravery", I decided to continue doing what I could to help raise awareness of this widespread and, in my opinion, still vastly under-represented topic.

As I ask people every time I post these words, if you can spare a few minutes, please read on. It might be important for you, or perhaps for someone you know. It's a short tale that may sound familiar.

THERE'S A MAN I know whose social anxiety is often so bad that sometimes he can't even answer his own front door. This is usually worse if he knows who's knocking. He would shake with fear. He'd become so twitchy and agitated that he would drop things and lock himself in the bathroom. He would sit on the floor and cry. Often when he tried to speak, he could hardly form a sentence.

On one occasion he spent three hours building up the courage simply to walk to a nearby corner shop, perhaps three hundred yards away. He was travelling at the time, and he didn't know anybody in the village. Yet, once he was finally brave enough to leave the hotel, and a stranger in a passing car honked and waved, his anxiety became so intolerable in that moment that he ducked behind a bush and waited for his anxiety-induced panic attack to pass. Thirty minutes later he emerged from hiding and trudged back to the hotel, still in tears. He never made it to the shop. Later that night was a good friend's much-anticipated 40th birthday fancy dress party, which is why he had travelled to be closer to the event. He missed the party because he was now too afraid to leave the house and catch the train. He couldn't tell any of his friends that were expecting him at the party why he didn't turn up, because he knew they wouldn't understand.

That level of anxiety can shadow him for weeks, sometimes months at a time. Most times this kind of "issue" happens — there have been hundreds and hundreds such incidents over the 30+

years he's suffered with it, more if you count his debilitating shyness at school — the guy is consumed with intensely burning skin, the itching so bad he regularly draws blood. He can't think straight, and becomes agitated, and confused with simple things. These bouts can last for many minutes, occasionally as long as an hour. There are often tears. The itching is a rare and very unfortunate by-product of his extreme anxiety. In public, it can be and often is a humiliating experience. It is his fear of these physical symptoms that can sometimes trigger the anxiety in the first place. Other times it's in reverse. He's not sure which way round is more powerful and more frightening, but they can both be crippling.

Until quite recently, the only way this man had ever really managed to control these "issues" that have traditionally come and gone in weeks, months, or even years-long spells, or at least get through it, was by using alcohol to suppress the anxiety. The drinking became so bad at times over some of those spells that he sometimes consumed a bottle of gin in the morning before going to work. When he went back to university in his early thirties, the first year was a blur of fear and alcohol.

Unfortunately, his two — somewhat reluctant — attempts at receiving professional help, once in his twenties and again in his thirties, didn't actually help at all, and in several periods the drinking threatened to derail him.

Finally, with the right medication over the last eighteen months, he has, in the main, managed to regain control over that darkness, and can now enjoy a drink for enjoyment's sake, though the fear of the medication no longer working, or the darkness randomly returning, is always there like a shadowy cloud on the horizon.

Sadly, in the past he suspected many of his old friends struggled to believe this rumour of secret alcohol abuse. Many people drink more than he does. But of course, it is the *need* to drink, not the *desire.* In truth, it doesn't matter what others believe. If this resonates with you, you likely already know that most high-functioning addicts or substance dependents are masters of disguise.

Neither this guy nor the doctors he's spoken to can really be sure what first caused this extreme form of social anxiety, though one doc recently told him he exhibited classic symptoms of PTSD, likely triggered by a couple of traumatic events in his younger years for which he never received counselling because, as like most of the UK, he was brought up to believe that counselling was for wimps. To clarify, the events were a parental divorce and a parent's sudden death, both while in his teens and both out of the blue.

Whatever the truth, it was certainly his social anxiety that initially caused the out-of-control drinking, and the drinking in turn later caused him to behave in ways he will always regret.

These "issues" have cost him friends and loved ones. They have cost him job opportunities and other life experiences. Both his mental and physical health have suffered immeasurably. When he's enduring a spell of continued anxiety, he often can't leave the house and exercise for months on end, which of course worsens his physical condition, and thus, it damages his state of mind. It's a vicious cycle. The health of the one improves the other, and vice versa. Conversely, when one is down, the other plummets along with it.

Simply stated, this awful form of social anxiety has dominated this man's life for much of the last three decades. There have even been times, albeit rarely, when he thought he simply couldn't take it anymore.

Luckily, it has never reached that extreme low point. Along with the medication he now takes daily and perhaps always will, and with heartfelt thanks to a few people who never judged him, and accepted him regardless of his weird, sometimes embarrassing situations, not to mention the mood swings and bouts of often unreasonable behaviour, in the last eighteen months he has managed to emerge from the unwelcome shade with a new-found passion for life, and especially recently, more days than not have been spent seeking out the light.

He had suffered in silence for so many years because he didn't want to burden people with his struggles, didn't want to make them uncomfortable and feel pity for him regarding his "issues".

Before the medication, he was often missing in action at times others thought he needn't be. Perhaps worse, in the times he felt better, he would make up for it, usually to ridiculous levels. It has caused him fights and fallouts, and periods of depression he found hard to shake off. He even neglected visiting family and close friends for long stretches. It was simply too stressful, and the fact he wasn't able to explain to them the reasons only exacerbated the problem. He has been considered aloof, rude, and even arrogant by friends and strangers alike. He has been ashamed about so many things for many years. He hopes that by sharing this, it might help explain a few of the reasons why.

Mercifully, in the guy's thirties there was a spell of close to eight years in which his anxiety "issues" randomly departed, though of course they were always lurking in the back of his mind. During those apparently halcyon days he was able to thrive and complete a triple university degree, and attain a CELTA teaching certificate, as well as teach English abroad for six years — things he could never have imagined in those darker times. He even appeared on a big international TV show, and there were also a couple of scary public book launch events that almost passed without incident. Almost. He was still so anxious, his amazing wife had to do his public reading for him while he hid behind a dozen glasses of wine.

So, it was a terrible day indeed when, nine years ago, totally — TOTALLY — out of the blue after those seven or eight anxiety-free years, his "issues" came back with a vengeance. It dealt him a devastating blow and set those dark clouds swirling again. He nearly faltered, nearly succumbed to the darkness and if it weren't for the support of his wife Leslie and the understanding of a few select friends, he's still not sure what would've happened.

THANK YOU FOR reading this far. You may or may not have worked it out, but that unfortunate guy was me. It is still me. Steven Moore. That "normal", apparently confident guy people thought they understood.

I continue to suffer from episodic bouts of extreme social anxiety, but the medication has been amazing — lifechanging — at keeping it under control. I am currently experiencing a social anxiety freedom I haven't had in years, and man does it feel good.

If you're reading this and have ever met me in person, you have probably spoken to me without having a clue of what I often deal with on a daily basis. There's a high chance I was dealing with it then. I am good at hiding it. Too good, I suppose. I suffered in silence all those years ago for the reasons stated above.

I first wrote about my issues for Mental Health Awareness Week in the UK a few years ago. Once I finally felt confident enough to emerge from my mental health closet, I decided I would try to become a kind of advocate for mental health awareness. I don't do a lot, but I do what I can. That's why I'm sharing this with you now.

Why? There was a time — the first two decades or more — when I didn't understand my own situation. I denied what should have been obvious... that I had mental health "issues". Instead, I judged other people for theirs and pretended I was just a bit "different", or just "extra shy".

In the last several years, a few people I have known — many of you will have known someone like them — have taken their own lives. I never saw it coming. I doubt you did either. More importantly, there's a good chance they themselves didn't believe it would ever reach such a tragic point.

People need to talk about their "issues" and share their burdens, but it is very difficult, and almost impossible for some of us. It was impossible for me for so long.

We as humans need to continue removing the outrageous stigma surrounding mental health and open up, both to ourselves, and to one another. It is the only way.

I am lucky. I have an extremely supportive wife who understands me and has always supported me. We all need to be as supportive as she has been, including myself.

Most of us cannot do it alone.

One of the greatest things this newfound freedom has given me is the ability to attend author events and other public gatherings without the need to get steaming drunk first. Until recently I lived abroad for a long time, almost twenty years, so even though I've been a novelist for a decade now, my first author events weren't until 2018. I went to the London Book Fair and one or two other similar events, but I was so nervous and anxious about them that by the time the events opened their doors, I'd already polished off at last a bottle and a half of wine and a few beers. Doors usually open at ten am. Then for me it's always... always... straight to the bar. It's the only way I can attend and it is NOT the way to make friends and influence people. Well, it is sometimes, of course, but you get my point.

Was I putting my best self forward? Was I doing myself proud? I never cause any problems and am always well behaved, but I would say, categorically, no, though I guess it's a question for others to answer. Weirdly, when people read about my struggles after they've met me a few times they tell me they are very surprised about my "issues" — both the anxiety and the drinking. They always say I seemed fun and "normal", when on the inside I felt like I was dying just trying to hold it altogether. Like I said, masters of disguise.

Now, however, with several author events this summer and beyond, I have no reason to fear. I trust in the medication, and I know that deep down, many authors are introverts, and as an avid reader myself, I know many readers are introverts, too.

As the cheesy title to this essay suggested, *I am you, you are me, we are altogether*. And I mean it. Together, we can help and encourage and support one another.

As I said, I am currently going through an amazing period of anxiety-free bliss. Thus, if you happen to see me at any other author events, or just in the pub sometime, please, do come and say hello. 99% of the time I will be delighted to speak to you. That 1%? Let me worry about that, and let's have a beer... or a glass of wine. I'm in control now, don't you know!

So, the next time you see someone who appears to be struggling mentally, give them your time, or if need be, lend them a shoulder to cry on. Don't judge them, and definitely don't ignore them, unless you are certain that is what they need. None of us know what "issues" each other is going through at any given moment. It can be so many different things, or it could be just one thing.

Spare a thought for them.

One day it might be you.

THANKS SO MUCH for reading and sharing in my story. And thank you Sarah for putting this inspiring collection together.

All the best,

Steven Moore

I SEE YOU

by Helen Bright

I wrote this poem for parents with children (whether teens or adults) who are suffering from clinical depression with suicidal thoughts. It can often be a thankless, lonely experience, even when you have support.

As you're sitting there wondering why,
why the child you adore wanted to die,
and why you never noticed the signs
as a dark depressive cloud took control of their mind

I See You

When you're wandering around in a daze,
as you navigate a world where you're so out of place,
and you suddenly feel so small,
climbing healthcare hurdles a thousand feet tall

I See You

While you're encouraging your child just to try,
try to eat, drink and bathe, get dressed, live their life
And when you're suffering through verbal abuse
because you questioned their rationale,
and their version of the truth

I See You

When you're scared to go out, just in case
that today is the day they've had enough of this place,
and you come home with fear in your heart,
each second of silence tearing your soul apart,

You shout out their name but receive no reply
So you bound up the stairs, two at a time
And you open their door with terrifying trepidation,
then cry with relief when you hear your name yelled in frustration...

Mum, what are you doing? I was sleeping.

Yes, I see you

I hear your silent screams,
know the tears that you hide
I feel all your pain,
see the world from your side

I respect your ability to get up and carry on
when every day is hell and their demons are strong,

When you see those posts on Facebook and the rest
that tell us to have compassion for those who are depressed,
and in your head, you're shouting out, "Why?"
Why there's no help for the families,
no step-by-step guide

So you muddle on through, doing your best,
taking care of those you love, no time for a rest

You want to ask for help
but you feel so ashamed
They might think it's your fault
and that you are to blame

I hugged them so much and showed them I cared.
But was I too strict, making life seem unfair?

WRITING IS OUR SUPERPOWER

You ask yourself questions,
time and time again
Your mind just won't stop,
it's no longer your friend

But you have to find peace,
lay all blame to rest
There'll be no judgement here
because I know you did your best

Depression is so random,
like the weather is in spring
Often no rhyme or reason
why it appears and does its thing

It can scare you, control you,
and knock you off your feet,
Steal your confidence and courage,
change your personality

Anyone can be a victim, and it can vary by degree
That monster can take many forms when it captures those it seeks
But whether a child, teen, or adult, there's no limit or age
where you could ever stop caring, you'd take all of their pain

Yet sometimes it's necessary to take a step back
You are their parent, not an unbreakable, verbal punchbag
You don't deserve to be attacked

It won't mean you don't love them or that you don't care
when you escape their all-consuming world of despair,

You can come back fighting,
gloves off this time
For them and for yourself
Self-care certainly isn't a crime,

And maybe, just maybe
they'll learn that from you,
love yourself as much as you love others,
though it's often hard to do

There is hope out there,
new treatments and care,
but it's an uphill battle too
So when the journey seems long, and you're travelling alone,
just remember, I see you.

AN ODE TO ADHD

by Rachel Dove

I want a big bright life but I don't want to burn,
I guess even at 40 I have a lot to learn
Burnout, anxiety,
not able to finish a drink of tea
Organising, fixating, paralysing, training
I aced school life but I liked my own company
A friend in need, let me at it

The pandemic hit and my brain said quit
The woman before wouldn't recognise me anymore
Failing, fear, I don't wanna be here
I just wanna get **** done
Be a good mum
You need me, that's OK Hun
I'll have your back,
If I remember to call you back

Stomach rumbling but I've got to get this done
Even though in the end I have to account to no one
Pressure pressure, all on me
I'm the only one who can set myself free
If only I could get a handle on my diary

Lists for days
Get Me Out of this maze
Special interests are my jam
I think I got it from my mam

***

THIS PIECE WAS ALMOST NEVER written. The ironic part is that I procrastinated so much on writing about my ADHD, that I had to force myself to sit and write down my thoughts before the deadline sailed past me. Something tells me a planner isn't going to combat this, but that's what the experts say. Keep life simple, don't clutter your house and life, be organised. Plan your day. The irony is that I crave routine, but then get bored. Such is life!

Growing up, I was always very emotional, heart on my sleeve, reactive. I always felt different from others growing up around me. Every other girl dreamed of marriage, or settling down into a career, or both. I watched my friends put on make-up, dress how they wanted, be authentically them. I never quite cared enough about any of that. I still don't. I still buy clothes I like, that are comfy. I loved my books, learning, and I didn't want to just do *one thing. I wanted to do everything!*

I had a few knocks in my life, and learned to rely on myself. You can't let you down, right?

My children were born, and I was teaching and writing on the side, when I had the time between bottles and studying and working. When my children were struggling, I recognised autism and they were both diagnosed. Later, my youngest son was also diagnosed with ADHD.

Autism I knew about, had qualifications and experience in the field. Hell, I taught adults *how* to help children with autism, how to change the school system to accommodate them.

ADHD, not so much. Both boys were like chalk and cheese, one a quiet reader, the other a loud social butterfly. I love them both equally and fiercely.

Life got busier, and people would say to me, 'How do you do it all? How are you so organised?' I'd shrug and say, 'It's not hard, it's just life!' I never forgot an appointment, never missed a deadline. I was flying, right?

Wrong.

I was, and have always been, looking back – a big ball of emotions and anxiety. I sleep only a few hours a night, figuring I was just a productive night owl. Nope.

When March 2020 hit, and the kids' school closed right when I had just won fighting for their education legally, I totally lost something. Me.

I couldn't cope. My routines had gone, the world seemed to be small and broken. I couldn't cope with the daily news, watching people around the world suffering, fighting. Already being isolated as a carer, life became hard. Deadlines got missed, and my emotions were something I couldn't trust anymore. I, overnight, stopped believing in myself. Therapy didn't help, and as the Verve famously said, the drugs don't work.

Whenever I have faced a problem in my life, I always did the same thing. I tried to solve it. I fell down a research rabbit hole, and my son showed me another answer. Was it just because I was actually neurodivergent? My boys were, and I loved and understood them. Could that be the key?

Armed with my research, I went down the diagnosis route. My long-suffering GP's face lit up. She knew as well as I did, this was the key to my life.

Being diagnosed at 41 was an eye opener. I wasn't too loud, too much, too sensitive. I was just...me. ADHD, but still me.

There is a period of reflection after diagnosis, and being diagnosed as an adult felt like getting an overlay to a map you never fully understood in the first place. A cheat sheet – why I reacted and acted like I did, why I saw the world so differently to other people.

Months on, I am on the right medication, the right diet. I don't burn out anymore, because I see the signs. Being 'on' all the time is not possible, for anyone, as much as we want it to be that way. I slept better, changed my working ways. I told people of my diagnosis. Their replies?

I don't know how you do it.

Dear reader, neither do I. But I do. Every day I wake up and get shit done. On the bad days, I don't beat myself up. We are all a work in progress, the way I see it, I'm just not finished yet. That's what life is for. Not a planner in the world can change my brain, and I wouldn't have it any other way. Now, when is that next deadline? Let me at it, world – I'm ready. Caffeinated, sleepy, slightly confused perhaps, but I'm ready.

GRIEF – THE PRICE OF LOVE

by Anna-Maria Athanasiou

"All deaths are sudden, no matter how gradual the dying may be."
– Michael McDowell

THE THING ABOUT DEATH IS that you know it's coming. It's not a surprise but yet when it comes to someone you love, it always feels like it's too soon. That is what grief feels like, that feeling that it came from nowhere, unexpectedly and so final.

I prepared myself for losing my dad. I saw the physical deterioration over time but that wasn't what made me start to prepare, it was when his will to live left him. I knew it was closer than I'd hoped. He'd lost part of himself gradually over time, his independence, his focus, his memory and worst of all, his fight.

My family had lost so many members in such a short space of time, six in four years, it felt like there wasn't enough time between each loss to recover, before the next came, and always unexpectedly. Each loss impacted parts of my family in different ways but for me it was the anticipation of the inevitability that utterly overwhelmed me.

I thought that preparing for loss would safeguard me from the grief. It was better than living in denial, something I'd witnessed in my family. They'd believed that they'd get better or that the symptoms of illness weren't worsening, and listening to them only made things so much harder. You're caught between not upsetting them more, and preparing them for what's to come. There's no right answer and at the same time you're having to navigate your own emotions.

I wasn't there when my dad died and I was told over and over, before and after he died that that would be something I'd be sad over, feel guilty about and always regret. It was unfortunately out of my control and the truth is, they were all wrong. I would've liked to have been there but for me, it was more important that my dad didn't suffer anymore. I'm forever thankful to my brother for my video call, where I got to see and speak to him a few days before he became unresponsive. We got to say the few words that will stay with me forever. My relationship with my dad didn't need me to be present, didn't need me to be close by. We communicated without words, without actions, we just knew.

No one can tell you how to grieve. I have felt totally alone in my grief and that is no reflection on my family and friends, it was my choice. No one will ever know another person's loss and pain, because each relationship is unique. But there is use in walking alongside one another and saying, 'I'm here, I'm listening.'

There's so much guilt connected to grief, 'Am I too sad?' or 'Am I not sad enough?' then 'I should be over it' or 'Why am I not done by now?' My experience has shown me that though it gets better, the experience is by no means linear, it goes forwards then backwards and often knocks you when you least expect it, and in my case, I still don't want to talk about it, I just want people to understand that it's constantly present, without vocalising it.

There's the guilt of forgetting them too; their voice, their walk, their laugh and the knowing that everything is still the same, yet different. That they won't be part of your life from now on and that thought still scares me.

WRITING IS OUR SUPERPOWER

EVERYONE DEALS WITH grief differently, vocalising, questioning, confirming their feelings. Some talk about their loved ones constantly, referring to them, as though talking about them means they won't be forgotten, or maybe they're worried they'll forget them, I really don't know. What I do know is that, I can't believe that I would ever forget my dad. I think about him every single day but I don't talk about him. I may refer to him, if the situation arises, but I don't actively talk about him. It's too personal. That's how I feel grief is, personal. And I don't want anyone to feel what I'm feeling because it's solely my pain to feel and bear.

It comes when I take my first sip of whisky, or when a Greek song comes on the radio. It comes when I drink a glass of water after eating minty chewing gum, the smell of newly printed material and when I see Easter egg cartons. All of these things are personal to me and I need a moment, an hour or a day to absorb the excruciating pain I feel and let it wash over me.

I've never wanted to share or show how heartbroken I was, which is why writing this piece seems strange and exposing. I'd listen to everyone talking about how they felt, what they were going through, how they dealt with things when they'd lost someone, and to be honest I didn't care. I don't mean that in an awful or disrespectful way. I just wanted everyone to not talk to me about it. I wanted them to understand that I wanted their silent support. It's a very rare gift to know how to react to a person in pain, and I've only met a handful of people in my whole life that understood that listening and sitting in silence is often all you need.

It's hard to sum up a person dying and then very slowly fading from your life. My dad was always very alive. I know that sounds ridiculous but he had a presence, for all his slight height and slim build, he still filled a room. He wasn't loud but somehow his stillness, steady voice and select words were heard. I can count the number of times he raised his voice on one hand, but yet people listened to him, he had that gift.

Loss makes you re-evaluate your life. You realise how precious and how short it is, and I know it's a cliché, but losing someone brings that to the fore. For me in the few weeks after my dad died, I found an inner strength to get things done, things I had put off. I finished writing a book, which had previously taken me forever to complete. It almost felt as though a fire had been lit under me, urging me to focus and finish it for him. My dad had never been a quitter, well not until the very end at least, and that was one of the hardest things to witness. It also made me stop obsessing over things beyond my control. I let things go.

The days before the funeral I became numb and strong for everyone who was crumbling around me. I ran on fumes and felt alone, even though I was surrounded by loved ones. I needed someone to just sit by me in silence, while I was utterly submersed in my grief. Sadly, the one person who could do that, was my dad. I was angry at everyone, disappointed at how everyone was just carrying on with their lives, how some were just being difficult, self-absorbed, how they made it all about them, that they seemed to be so thoughtless and just wouldn't stop talking. Everything was just, too much, until a cousin and a close friend took one look at me and said, 'Don't worry, we've got you.' Nothing more. They gave me permission to break down and let out my anger, without saying a word. Because I was so angry. No one talks about the extreme anger you feel, it felt like a blind rage, and for someone who rarely feels such an extreme, uncontrollable emotion, it was terrifying.

It's twenty months since my dad died and yes, I'm still counting the months. It still feels like it did in the first few weeks. I read somewhere that time doesn't heal, but it does allow you to make choices about how you present your pain, and I find that to be so true. Grief is like the sea, the waves keep coming, sometimes they gently nudge you, other times they crash over you and all you can do is to bury your feet in the sand, to withstand their force. But it will never go. Even the gentle lapping that tickles your ankles, but you learn to live with it and hope that one day, the sea stays calm.

SOCIAL ANXIETY & PANIC ATTACKS

by Nicola Rose

I'D LIKE TO TELL YOU something that I couldn't tell a single soul about for many years. I went through a mental health crisis alone, too embarrassed to tell anyone: not my boyfriend, best friends, or family. Not even a doctor. I faced it alone and, thankfully, I came out the other side. But now? Now I'll tell anyone who'll listen because I've learned that there is *nothing* to be ashamed of and we *should* talk about these things. I'm here to remind you that if you're struggling, no matter what the issue may be, connecting with others is surely one of the best therapies? You might be surprised by just how many other people are going through the same thing. But if you're still not ready for that, then perhaps reading my story might at least be helpful and comforting in some way.

I suppose it begins in my childhood when my grandad died and then my nan came to live with us. It wasn't really because she was too old to cope on her own, but more because of her mental health.

She was severely agoraphobic.

In our home, she was given her own room and bathroom on the ground floor. Despite that being right next to the living room, I rarely saw her. Not only did she never leave the house, but rarely even the sanctity of her room. *She stared at those four walls for over a decade.*

As a child, I didn't understand. None of the family really did. I think we all found it a bit frustrating. I remember trying to take her on holiday with us one year (within the UK), but literally within minutes of arriving (we hadn't even left the car park) she was so upset that my dad had to drive her back home. I don't think we even tried to take her anywhere again after that.

I carry quite a bit of guilt around now — for not going and sitting with her, talking to her, listening to her life stories. But I was a child, and then a teenager, and by the time I'd grown up enough to realise that just because she didn't come and sit with the family, it didn't necessarily mean she didn't want some company, that I should have gone into her room and spent more time with her, she was gone.

As a child I was a little shy and nervous. I wasn't popular at school and hated any attention on me. I lacked self-confidence and generally avoided new or daunting social situations.

YET WHEN I hit sixteen, a switch flipped. I started going out, partying, attracting attention, and I found my confidence. Cue years of clubbing and drinking, loving the active social life of a young adult.

It was all great until around twenty-five years old. After a six month break up from my then boyfriend (now husband) we had just got back together. I was happy in my job, my life, all was good.

One day we were out shopping in the town centre when we bumped into my old boss from a previous job. We made polite small talk. And for some reason I suddenly felt a bit embarrassed and awkward. I don't remember why. It was probably related to the fact that my boyfriend and I had met at that workplace and both of us had since moved to other employment — but the last my boss had known was that we'd separated. She was delighted to see us back together, but we'd literally only just re-united the previous week or something and I guess I felt a bit self-conscious having to discuss it in the middle of the shopping centre with someone I hadn't expected to see. I felt myself going red. Then I was struggling to focus on the conversation. I got dizzy and clammy. Heart racing. Hands trembling.

We finished the chat and off we went. I'm not sure if my boyfriend even noticed or not, I don't think we mentioned it, but I felt like the conversation had been painfully awkward and like I must have looked ridiculous, dithering and panicking and blushing for no reason.

I got home and felt awful. I was mortified by this weird experience!

I can't remember precisely what incident happened next, but there was a similar situation where I was out in public, talking to someone, and I felt the same thing happening again. Days later, I then found it happening when I was talking to people at work. Followed by my own brother! Then my boyfriend.

I was spiralling. It played on my mind so much that all I could think about was how stupid I looked every time I started feeling panicky when people spoke to me.

And then *BOOM*. I was in my bedroom having the biggest panic attack of my life. I thought I was literally dying. I'm talking uncontrollable sobbing, barely able to breathe, feeling like I was having a heart attack. It was horrendous. Crushing pain and pressure in my chest, a frightening sense of doom.

Afterward, sitting there completely drained, I knew exactly what was going on.

One word kept haunting me.

Agoraphobia.

Suddenly, I was terrified of leaving the house. I felt certain that I'd have more attacks. The idea of any sort of social situation where I might bump into someone and have to talk to them filled me with horror. I just knew a panic attack would surface and I'd want the ground to swallow me up.

So, I stayed home.

I called in sick to work. I told my boyfriend I was sick.

I hid in my bedroom. Staring at the four walls.

Every night I went to bed with my heart racing and a sense of dread looming over me. And every morning I woke up feeling the same. But after a week, I couldn't keep making excuses that I was ill. I was going to have to go to work.

I'd been thinking a lot about my nan as I cried in my room.

I was going to turn into my nan.

If I didn't do something to fix this problem, that would be it. From the young age of mid-twenties, I would cease to live. I'd stop leaving the house entirely and I'd live in solitude forever. It was so frightening how suddenly and severely it had come on, seemingly out of nowhere and for no real reason. If it was already this bad, what would it be like in a years' time? In ten years?

I couldn't become my nan.

I *wouldn't* let that happen.

Because I also thought of my mum whilst I sat staring at those walls as they closed in on me, and I drew strength from who she had been. She was a glass half full person. In fact, she was the most optimistic and positive person I've ever known. I never heard her complaining. No matter what she faced through ten years of recurring cancer, she always smiled. Unfortunately, she lost the battle when I was seventeen.

"What would she do?" I asked myself as my life began sliding away into a murky, anxious place.

She'd get up and fight, of course.

She'd smile, laugh, and spread her joy. She had so many friends, and she ran a cancer support group to help others. She was the sun. People orbited her, bathing in her warmth.

After she died, her workplace had a plaque made up in memorial, and under her name it said — "Crisis? What crisis?!"

Nothing rattled her.

I'm not as amazing as she was, but I have always firmly believed that things will always turn out OK in the end. I rarely let anything bother me. I don't stress or get upset about things. I let it wash over me and trust that even if something isn't great today, it'll work out.

The suddenness and ferocity of this mental health crisis was alarming, but I clung to these things. I held on to my mum's strength and positivity, and I stubbornly refused to suffer the fate of my nan.

Yet, this being 2004 when there wasn't the huge online presence and resources of today, when these things didn't seem to be talked about so openly, I was too scared or embarrassed to call the doctor or tell anyone what I was going through. Instead, I quietly ordered a self-help book on dealing with anxiety. I read it cover to cover. It felt SO good to understand more about what I was going through and to know that I could help myself. This didn't have to be a terrible slippery slope into a breakdown.

That book taught me the most valuable lesson — the power of distraction. Trust me, it was *huge*!

Sure, I learned about how it really is just all in our head, mind over matter. How when we feel nervous about going into a situation in case we have an anxiety attack, that we should think about that happening, work out the worst-case scenario and realise that it likely won't even be that bad.

But I also learned that once you're in that situation and you begin to feel the anxiety surface, the key is distraction, distraction, *distraction*. I'm sure the book taught me many other things too, but I don't remember them now.

All I remember is knowing that if I felt an attack coming on, I must divert my attention somewhere else instead of falling into the spiral of worrying about what was happening and making it worse. Not to care if my cheeks were red. So what? It didn't matter. Racing heart? Who cares. It was just a physical reaction, and I could take back control.

It sounds simple and obvious, but it changed my life and diverted the course I was on. I learned to distract myself with anything I could – maybe I'd suddenly start thinking about what to cook for dinner, or what my favourite colour was, anything other than the anxiety I was feeling.

And if that wasn't working, then I would remove myself from the situation.

With me, the anxiety attacks nearly always happened when I was talking to someone. I would suddenly become too aware of myself, feel like my voice was odd, that I was blushing, or losing my train of conversation, and so I learned to simply quit the conversation. It was abrupt, and likely seemed a bit weird to the other party, but if we were talking and I felt the need to escape I'd blurt out, "I'm really sorry, I've got to go to the toilet! I can't wait!"

I'd scurry off to the loo. Give myself a pep talk. Calm down. Then I'd go back out and carry on.

I'd recover the conversation and be fine.

This was victory! And victory is powerful. Because with each victory, every time I successfully diverted an anxiety attack, I grew more confident. I knew I could handle it, no matter what.

And what came on the back of that?

Less anxiety!

I'm fortunate enough that I managed to squash these panic attacks fairly quickly, within weeks. I never had another huge one. And the little ones were stopped in their tracks. I carried on living my life. That's not to say it was smooth sailing. I think I probably still spent a year or so with a ripple of anxiety under the surface. I was still going to bed with a racing heart and waking up the same. But I managed to ignore it and put myself out there.

Eventually, I didn't even have to think about any of it anymore.

It seems so sad to me now that I couldn't tell anyone at the time because here, today, I'm more than happy to tell anyone, *everyone*. But maybe that's because I made it through the other side. Maybe if I was still having the same issues, I'd still be trying to hide it? I'd like to think not. Mental health awareness is much more open these days.

Anyway, if my story can help just one person, someone who can relate and is going through what I did, that I can shine them a light, show the way to hope and recovery, then I'll keep on talking.

Writing isn't the superpower that helped me through *my* journey, I wasn't writing back then, but it's the one that I can certainly use now – freely talking about my experience without any of the shame I once felt, and hopefully helping others to realise they can do the same on *their* journey.

I wonder, if I'd just told my work colleagues, friends, and family what was going on, maybe recovery could have been even easier? If, instead of having to make an excuse and dash off to avoid an attack,

I could have just laughed and so, "Oh, I'm sorry, I'm feeling a bit anxious right now! I just need a minute."

Then again, to this day, I still very occasionally feel a slight anxiety rising — and I still just lean back on my old tactics of distracting my mind and I carry on. Even though I'll happily tell people what I went through, I still very much talk about it in past tense and never present.

Maybe writing this down and putting it out there is the power I need to take that final leap into total acceptance of living with a level of anxiety without a shred of shame.

For anyone interested, I don't have the book any longer, but I'm pretty sure the one that helped me is called *The Anxiety Toolbox* by Gloria Thomas.

LOVE & DISORDER

by Eleanor Lloyd-Jones

I'VE BEEN AROUND PEOPLE WHO struggle with their mental health since I was about seven years old. There was a time when I wondered if I attracted it—if perhaps people navigated towards me for whatever reason or if I subconsciously sought them out. Turns out, so many more people than we realise battle every day, and sometimes we never even know.

My first encounter with mental health conditions was my mum's schizophrenia. Growing up witnessing how it affected her was harrowing to say the least. The illness took my mum away from me, from us, mentally and physically. My family was torn apart because of it but, until I was about eighteen, I didn't understand why. My dad did what he thought was best in an unprecedented situation, working so hard to give us a stable, loving childhood, protecting us from a lot of the horrors he was faced with—including my mum being sectioned. He paid privately for medical care and saved as much money as he could on his newly qualified teacher's wages, offering it to the doctors and asking the question, "Will this be enough to bring her back to me?" No one really understood, and no one knew how to 'fix' her, not even two thousand pounds worth of medical insight.

We did have a stable, loving childhood and in the midst of it, we gained a beautiful, supportive stepmother who loved us like we were her own and still does. But we weren't completely protected from this cruel illness. It affected us deep to our cores and went a long way towards shaping us into the people we are today.

I got a phone call in 1990. My brother was in crisis mode. We all travelled to see him in his home. He was having a breakdown. None of us really knew what it was or why he was having it, not even him, but years later he was diagnosed with anxiety. During lots of discussions and heart-to-hearts, we dug deep as a family and our past came spilling out of dark corners. It transpired that my brother had no living memory of our family before my parents split up due to the trauma caused by Mum's schizophrenia. Dad opened up for the first time since my mum's diagnosis. He told my brother things he'd kept from us to protect us and helped him to fill the gaps. My brother and I met to talk through our shared childhood experience and discovered we had developed similar coping mechanisms and that we were both aware we'd been affected more than we'd thought.

My dad and I talked, too, but not until I was 48 years old. It was the first time I was ever made privy to the way he had been affected and how my brother and I had reacted to and coped with living with a mother with a mental health condition. I learned that we had been impeccably behaved at all times, and that we'd developed what my dad described as, "an incredible resistance to disappointment." We learned to cope with being let down due to plans being cancelled; Mum would often fall apart at the last minute or be too ill to go anywhere or do anything.

"I mastered the art of making alternative plans sound even more appealing than the real thing. I remember looking down at you both, your big eyes wide with anticipation, when I told you, 'We're not going camping anymore, we are doing something even better... We're having

a carpet picnic at home. Yay!' You both would always join in the excitement I feigned."

I WOULD KNOW instinctively that Mum had gone back into hospital every time my dad would pick us up from school. She was in and out over many years. Sometimes we'd visit her, but mostly we were looked after by friends or family members and kept well away from schizophrenia.

I remember being fifteen years old and it being a weekend at Mum's. I'd had a bad feeling about it before it had even started. I still hadn't been made aware of the full extent of the illness, but I'd always been able to read my dad and could tell he had been worried about leaving us. A trip to Chester Zoo had been planned, which should have been easy really. It meant being out of the house with things to talk about instead of the uncomfortable, painful silence I was often met with when trying to communicate with her. I remember going to bed with a knot in my stomach anyway, leaving Mum in the kitchen stressing over picnic food that she'd planned way too far in advance.

Talking to her years later, I asked her why she would always fuss about food, over-preparing and worrying about it—making sure we ate, sometimes forcing us to. She admitted that having had her children essentially taken away from her because she was unable to care for us had been the worst part of the illness, and each time she was given the chance to be a mother, she wanted to prove she was a good one.

The journey to the zoo was one I'll never forget. It's burned into my memory as one of the first times I'd witnessed what I now know was unusual behaviour.

"One of the things you need to look out for is when she starts to laugh inappropriately. This is a good sign that she is not well."

My dad's words had reverberated in the back of my mind when my mum started to laugh, seemingly out of nowhere in the car. I'd pushed them to the side giving her the benefit of the doubt, but I had known there and then that we were going to have a difficult day.

"What are you laughing at?"

She snaps her head around to try to look at me. "Nothing."

I challenge her, mainly because I need to know what I am dealing with here.

"What do you mean nothing? Something must be funny." I'm glad she can't see my face, because I don't think it would help matters.

"I can laugh if I want to, can't I? Don't have to be laughing at anything funny." She is unreasonably angry with my comments.

My brother didn't understand the situation at all until many years later. He'd found not being with her incredibly difficult and at times had to be prised away from her when my dad had come to pick us up. It was heart-breaking seeing him like that, seeing Mum destroyed, seeing Dad trying to keep everything together.

And for that reason, I had often dreaded our visits with Mum. I'd dreaded them because I hadn't known what I was going to be faced with or how many egg shells I was going to have to step over.

Another vivid memory I have is being around sixteen years old. My mum was hunched and rigid on the sofa, a shell of the strong, beautiful woman I'd clung to as a small child. I remember feeling helpless, irritated and out of my depth. I'd had revision to do for my GCSEs but I couldn't bear to leave her alone.

The voices tell her that horrible things will happen to her. She won't go swimming because of them, and she won't ride a train.

Once, they told her my auntie was a cannibal. She even locked herself in the house for days because of them, after they told her there was a war going on outside her front door.

I couldn't even begin to understand that back then, and still can't.

I used to shout at her to ignore them, to block them out. I wished for her not to be so 'weak'. I'd tell her there's no such thing as 'voices'. But I knew the fear was real for her—I knew because I'd been able to see it in her eyes.

I hadn't known what was expected of me as a teenager. It was adult stuff.

I want to climb inside her head, to shut off the sad switch.

"Please smile." I search her eyes for a glimmer of the bright, full-of-life mother from my early years, but I don't see even a flicker of light, and I know what's coming next.

She holds my gaze with her dull, lifeless stare. "I can't, Becca."

I give her a sideways glance before I curl my feet up, gently pulling her body towards me, and I try to embrace her wooden frame.

If I hold her, if I keep her close to me, then maybe my love for her will permeate her being and be enough to fight the demon that is wrapped around her soul.

I want my mum back.

Mum is seventy-one now and really very happy. She's remarried and her treatment has meant she has been stable for many years. We have advancements in medicine to thank for that.

It has been a tremendously long haul to reach this point and for her to be able to say, not that she's completely beaten it, but that she is living a very purposeful life in spite of it.

Her mornings are heavy and tiring due to medication, which she says seems to do its job.

Instead of sleeplessness and clinging onto her bed in fear and trepidation, she now sleeps well and gets up early, dressed in clothes that are picked and laid out the night before in an attempt to achieve some sort of routine. It helps her a great deal to get out in the air in the mornings, and riding on the local bus takes her to various shops and to friends. She loves to browse the charity shops and it gives her a real lift when she finds a bargain.

The voices are still there, still horrendous, and she finds it hard to concentrate. When she talks back to them, tells them to leave her alone, they reply viciously and change her thoughts. Anxiety can rear its ugly head very suddenly for ridiculous reasons and she can still fall into low feelings. She has been scarred forever on the horrendous journey of mental illness. It's a fight every day still, but she's not afraid of the future now.

However, it still makes me incredibly sad that she lost so much of her young life to this crippling illness—that we lost her, too.

In the late 90s, I was in a relationship with a man who had been diagnosed with bipolar and manic depression. I was right in the midst of this and witnessed what it did to him on a daily basis. Through rose-coloured spectacles, we were happy but, looking back it was more that I'd been desperate for us to be without really understanding what having me in his life was doing to him. He would sleep all day, and of course when he woke, I wanted his time. He obliged, but really what he'd needed was time for himself.

The whole house had been covered in pieces of A4 paper that had handwritten lists and notes on them to remind him of things his incredibly clever and troubled mind kept him up all night overanalysing.

Maintaining the relationship was impossible and it broke my heart when he told me he had no room in his head for me. The relationship only lasted a year, despite us loving each other so very much. The illness was debilitating in a way that meant all of his energies were focused on trying to get through each day. Having me there trying to be supportive and getting in the way of his coping mechanisms was too difficult and I believe made things worse. Twenty-five years on, he is still single, still won't drive but has figured out a routine that has kept him as stable as he can be. He used to spend his spare time filling his mind with new information, building computers, writing songs and listening to music. He would seek activities that kept his mind busy. Now he doesn't listen to any music that has words, he no longer owns a computer. He turns his phone off at lunchtime and doesn't communicate with anyone after midday. This simple life he lives calms the whirring of his over-stimulated brain and allows him peace. What a beautiful, talented and intelligent man he is but one whose potential was snatched away from him without permission at the tender age of nineteen.

I am now in a relationship that has somehow lasted seventeen years. It is one that has been riddled with ups and downs and difficult times due to what we now know as undiagnosed anxiety and depression—his, not mine. He has also had a diagnosis of autism, and we are currently navigating what life is going to look like from here on out. For a very long time, he masked and mirrored and coped, using alcohol and coffee to get him through each day. He wouldn't ever open up to me about his feelings and it caused friction and fall outs on a regular basis.

We are nowhere near the end of this very long road we are travelling, but him accepting that it is okay to not be okay, means we are closer than ever and in a much better place. We are now talking;

he can tell me how he is feeling and I can understand his behaviours better.

Since writing is my superpower, I've considered an autobiographical fiction novel to try to sort through my feelings and thoughts about everything: the experiences I've had, the way I've processed them and how I've handled the many tribulations thrown in my path.

I haven't managed it yet.

BECOMING MYSELF

by Jamie Luna

HELLO, MY NAME IS JAMIE, but you may know me as Mr Luna. I thought this would be a great opportunity to write about my experience with mental health.

To look at me now, I may come across as a happy-go-lucky guy. But it's taken a lot of hard work for me to get to this stage. I've had to battle my inner demons on a regular basis, trying not to succumb to them. Men have always been told to "man up" and to just bottle up our emotions, as it's not seen as masculine to admit we're struggling with our mental health. So a lot of men don't bother to get the help they desperately need. I was almost one of those men.

Depression and suicidal thoughts are something I've had to deal with on a daily basis for as long as I can remember, but I'm thankful I ignored the stigma around men getting help with mental health issues, as it's stopped me from entertaining those dark, depressive thoughts, and it most likely saved my life.

My childhood was pretty normal. I had a loving family, and grew up with my sister, who's a year older. My parents brought me up well, and did their best to provide for me. I was a happy child, but I would always worry a lot. I remember telling my mum when I was only eight years old that I don't want to get married when I'm older because everyone will be staring at me and I'll forget what to say.

WRITING IS OUR SUPERPOWER

Even as a child, one of my biggest fears in life was people thinking I was stupid. I would be terrified when I had to talk to people in case I messed up my words and they would laugh at me.

This then actually happened to me when I was around twelve years old. I was trying to tell another kid something, but I was having trouble trying to pronounce a particular word, and kept saying it incorrectly. Most people would laugh it off, but this was a big deal to me as I'm constantly trying my hardest not to come across as dumb. Now the other kid wasn't being overly mean, but I felt he was mocking me, as he just started laughing and repeating my mistake back to me. For some reason, this incident stuck with me and reconfirmed my belief that I was stupid, and that I was better off just being quiet. It's amazing what effect such a small interaction can have on your life, when someone makes a comment on that one thing you're ultra-sensitive about. I then put even more pressure on myself whenever I had to talk, as I believed it would lead to being mocked again

During my teenage years, I developed two conditions that I didn't realise I had until I was around thirty years old. One is called silent acid reflux, which doesn't sound too bad, but it had such a negative impact on my life. Stomach acid would coat my voice box, and after just a few minutes of talking, my throat felt inflamed and sore, and I had to really strain my vocal cords to produce any sort of sound. This made the social anxiety I had developed over the years so much worse, as I was scared to talk due to the pain I got from speaking, and I was convinced people would hear me struggle and call me stupid.

The second condition is called idiopathic hypersomnia, which is a sleeping condition. It basically means that no matter how much sleep I get at night, I will still be exhausted the next day. It felt like I hadn't actually slept for two days each time I woke up. Battling depression and anxiety when feeling fully awake is difficult enough, but trying to do it when exhausted is on a whole new level. When suicidal thoughts linger in the back of your mind, mental clarity can really help to fight it. However, when you're so exhausted mentally, it's easy to listen to those inner demons and be overcome.

As I grew into adulthood, my anxiety decided to keep following me around like a shadow, and I was just constantly preparing myself for the worst-case scenario. It got to the point where I was so fed up with feeling anxious all the time, I decided to do something about it. My thought process was to face my fears by socialising more with friends, and even work colleagues, on nights out. But, man, did I struggle. I just wanted to be like everyone else, chipping into conversations, making jokes to make others laugh. But when I tried it, I was just... awkward.

On the off chance I got a chuckle, my first thought was to repeat the same sort of joke again, hoping to get the same reaction, but I just created awkward silences. I was so envious of how everyone was able to join in with conversations naturally, while there was me, sitting there getting overwhelmed at the mere thought of having to say something.

At the end of the night, when I was lying in bed, I would go through every single conversation, critiquing every sentence I had said throughout the course of the evening. This would happen after every social event, and it was just so draining. In the end, I decided I was better off with my own company. I had this mindset for quite a few years. It was a very lonely period.

I tried so hard to fight my daily battle with anxiety and depression by "manning up", but I didn't get the results I desperately wanted. So, I decided to reach out for help, and went to see my GP. He kindly put me through to a mental health team where I tried CBT therapy for the first time.

I quite enjoyed my one-on-one sessions. It was really nice to have someone just listening to me for an hour a week, that wouldn't butt in or cut me up mid-sentence. They would actually listen and be interested in what I had to say. This did start to help with my social anxiety, as it was challenging my way of thinking, and trying to show me that talking to another person isn't the big deal that I had geared it up as in my head. This is harder than it sounds though, as you're trying to undo years of thinking a particular way. It's like going from a beer belly to a six pack. It won't happen overnight, and will take a lot of sessions to get there.

To put my new way of thinking into practice, I even tried giving dating a go. I went on dating websites and did my best to impress the opposite sex. Being a short guy is tough when it comes to dating, as most women are after that tall, dark, and handsome man, or even that elusive bad boy. I was hardly a catch, as I was extremely underweight, I had no self-confidence, and I was scared to talk to people. Then, even if I did talk, I could only manage around twenty minutes maximum before my vocal cords decided they'd had enough. But, shockingly, there were a few girls who were interested.

I tried taking my dates bowling or to the cinema. The theory behind this was that I hoped they would have a fun evening without me having to talk too much. But, in reality, it wasn't a good plan, as we never really got to know each other, and would always go our separate ways at the end of the evening.

At this stage in my life, I was at one of my lowest points. I had pushed all my old school friends away, and I couldn't make new friends. No girls were interested in me. I had hit rock bottom. I felt I had absolutely no purpose in life. That's when my thoughts darkened, and I thought that life would be so much easier if I wasn't here anymore. Horrible thoughts started to enter my head and I tried to work out which method would be the easiest and least painful. It hurts now to talk about how bad things got, but I think not talking about it was part of the problem.

Knowing I couldn't succumb to these thoughts—mainly as I couldn't hurt my mum in that way—I continued to do my CBT sessions, in the hope it would help. After an additional month of sessions, I felt they were starting to help. They were trying to change my thought process, making me see things in a more positive view. This is not a quick process, as it's trying to undo years of negative thinking. I used anxiety as a safety blanket to a degree, to avoid putting myself out of my comfort zone, and that needed to change.

At the end of each CBT session, I was assigned a homework task, and it was then up to me to try and complete it by the next session. Whenever we had a new member of staff at work, I would normally have kept quiet and not said anything to them, but this time, I pushed myself to start up a conversation—which was my CBT homework. I introduced myself and asked what their name was, and I made small talk for five minutes.

Now, I know how pathetic this sounds, but I was so proud of myself. I had pushed myself out of my comfort zone and nothing bad had happened. Plus, the new staff member looked really happy that I had gone over to talk to her, as she was sitting by herself. This was a small step in the right direction.

A few weeks after this event, I started to think about what things I've always wanted to do. Now could be the perfect time to do them, while I'm pushing myself. So, I decided I wanted to travel to America, to see all the amazing things it had to offer. However, I was not so brave as to travel by myself. So, after a few Google searches, I found a website called *Trek America*. It looked perfect. There's a trek leader who takes you across the country from New York to LA over a three-week period, and I'd be travelling with other lone travellers. I thought this was perfect as they would be in the same position as me, and it would be a good chance to make new friends.

The first day went well, as we were all rather nervous, and I used my new skillset to help me make small talk with everyone. This excitement soon soured quickly, and after the first week, I wanted to come home. I just wanted to fit in, but when you're socially awkward, it's easy to try too hard and end up saying the wrong thing.

After a few days, we had started to form our own little friendship groups. I felt like the black sheep, as I wasn't part of anyone's inner circle. I noticed people were making jokes and taking the piss out of each other, as a way to bond. Feeling like I had read the room correctly, I decided I should make an effort and said something jokingly to someone, the same way everyone else was, but they took it as an insult, which was never my intention. I felt people didn't like me after that, and it undid all the confidence I had been working so hard to build up. I pulled away from them all after that, and stopped even trying to make friends.

By the end of the trip, I barely got a goodbye from anyone, and a year later, they had a reunion in London. I did not get an invite.

After my holiday, I went back to being a recluse, not wanting to socialise with anyone. I felt I was stuck between a rock and a hard place. I wanted to be by myself, but at the same time, I was so lonely. My thoughts were very conflicting, but the idea of having a girlfriend sounded wonderful. Someone who would like me for me, and who would be interested in what I'd been up to.

So, I decided to give dating another shot. Sadly, I was getting the same sort of results as before. I wasn't someone who was being extremely picky and rejecting everyone. I just wanted someone who was genuinely interested in getting to know me. To see that beyond the nervous persona, there was someone with a fun personality, who cared a lot, and wanted to get to know them, too.

Something I learned from CBT is that conversation is like a tennis match, both people should be joining in, and the conversation should go back and forth.

However, I found the women I was talking to at the time, they just wanted to talk about themselves. Conversation tennis isn't fun when you have to stand there, not being allowed to return the serve.

One day I got a message from someone. You may know her; her name is Emma Luna. As we got chatting, I soon realised she was the master of conversation tennis. She actually took an interest in what I had been up to, and she really wanted to get to know me.

I even checked my dating profile to make sure I hadn't accidentally put my height as six foot five. Nope, turns out I had put five foot five, and she was still talking to me.

After a few weeks, we were gearing up to go on our first date. Then, as it was fast approaching, Emma told me she had broken her foot. I was convinced she only said this as an excuse to get out of going on the date. My self-doubt and insecurities convinced me she was trying to end things, so I moved on and we ended up chatting to other people.

A few weeks later, I went on another date with another girl. Again, it just didn't work out. I was so deflated at this point and felt like giving up. I just wasn't cut out for the dating world. As this realisation hit me, my depression seeped in, and I hit another low period. The thought of being alone for the rest of my life was terrifying, and yet, at the same time, I thought being by myself would be easier. There was no winning, as the dark thoughts clouded my judgement.

Then, later that night, out of the blue, I got a text message. It was from Emma. My eyes lit up and I had a massive smile on my face. We started messaging again, and it was just like before. It was so nice having someone who was genuinely interested in what I'd been up to, and what I had to say. If you're a fan of the show *Friends*, you'll understand this quote: *I had found my lobster*.

My life would be very different now if I hadn't met Emma. Maybe I wouldn't even be here at all? She has helped me so much over the last ten years. She encouraged me to go back to mental health services, to undertake more CBT therapy, and I finally got prescribed medication for my anxiety and depression. I'm so much happier since I've been on it.

It took well over a year of trying different types of antidepressants to find some that worked, and sometimes I wanted to give up. I just wanted to take a magic pill that would cure me, but with mental health, it's not that simple, and that was one of the hardest things I had to get my head around. I, for some reason, got it into my head that if I was given medication for anxiety, suddenly my whole personality would change and I would become an ultra-confident person, be happy all the time, and never have a bad day. The sad truth is that it doesn't work like that. I still have bad days, and I have to put in a lot of effort daily. But I'm now at the stage where I'm happy with who I've become as a person.

The medications I currently take are Quetiapine and Clomipramine. They suppress all the nervous energy I had bubbling under the surface. It's not perfect, as it does seem to make me more forgetful. Emma will often say in conversation, "Remember when we did this?" and I have absolutely no memory of it. But, to be honest, I will take these side effects over being anxious and depressed.

All I had to do now was sort out this issue with my vocal cords hurting continuously. I think my GP was sick of me coming to see him at this point, and he arranged for me to see an ear, nose, and throat specialist—which turned out to be a very important appointment. I had a camera inserted down my nose, into my throat, to finally see what the issue was. It sounds horrible, but I was actually really excited to have this done. Finally, I'd find out what had been causing this issue. I was hoping they would find something just so they could give me treatment and cure it, once and for all. And you know what they found... Nothing!

How could this be? I knew I wasn't imagining this constant pain. I was utterly distraught. The consultant calmed me down and explained he had found nothing serious, but that my throat and vocal cords did look slightly inflamed, which could be caused by silent acid reflux. I was still upset, as I was convinced I had something seriously wrong, but at least they were going to provide me with medication to try to tackle it. He seemed sure it would work, but I was sceptical. And to my surprise, the medication, called Lansoprazole, was like a miracle cure.

That stuff is amazing! After a few days of taking it, I no longer had inflamed vocal cords. Finally, I could talk with no discomfort.

This was a very happy moment in my life. It has since helped me gain enough confidence to apply for a job in IT, which is something I've always wanted to do. And over the last four years working for the NHS, I've had two promotions.

So the best advice I could give is to not be afraid to get help. This is a perfect time too, as the government has finally put some money towards helping mental health services—though a lot more is needed. So there's never been a better time.

Secondly, get enough sleep. I can't stress how important this is. Having a sleep condition has made my recovery ten times harder. I'm thankful I went to the doctor about my extreme tiredness, as I got referred to a specialist sleep clinic where I was finally diagnosed with idiopathic hypersomnia. I'm now on medication called Dexamfetamine, which I take in the morning to help me wake up. It helps bring my energy levels up to normal so I can function correctly, just like everyone else. But I still have to make sure I get a solid nine to ten hours of sleep per night.

I've found sleep to be an essential part of my routine, and having a healthy sleep routine is something my sleep specialist constantly drills into me. So, now I can't stress this enough. Even though I would love nothing more than to stay up playing my PlayStation until 2am on a work night, I know I would be incapable of working the next day. So, do take this seriously and be well rested. Find a sleep routine that works for you, and stick to it each and every night.

Lastly, don't be put off from taking medication. The amount of people who said to me, "Oh you don't need to be on that." The truth is, I'd be lost without it. Yes, the side effects can be scary, but that's something you have to weigh up for yourself. Which can you live with? The symptoms you were having, or the side effects? For me it was an easy choice, but that was me.

But, of course, the decision is always yours. You have to do what's best for you, but you don't have to do it alone. Suicide is one of the number one causes of death amongst young guys here in the

UK. That shouldn't be a statistic. All you have to do is find that one person you trust, and talk to them. One day, having someone by your side really could save your life. I know it did for me.

Thank you to everyone who's made it this far. If you too are struggling with mental health, I really hope you manage to get all the help you need. Though the future may seem bleak now, it won't always be. There was a time when I didn't even think I had a future. Now I'm living with the woman I love, we're getting ready to buy a house together, and I see a future where I grow old with her. You can have any future you want, just give yourself the chance.

Thanks for reading. I look forward to seeing everyone at all the future book signings.

FRIENDS WITH MY MONSTER

by Emma Luna

IF YOU'D ASKED ME A few years ago, I would have told you I was an expert in all things mental health. I trained as a midwife, and I've cared for women experiencing all manner of mental illnesses.

I looked after a woman who was so deep in her postnatal psychosis that she didn't even know she'd had a baby most of the time, and when she did recognise him, she thought he was a demon sent by the devil to kill her. I had to learn not only how to communicate with her, and understand what she was going through, but also come up with ways to care for them both without putting them in danger.

That was just one example, and no matter how scary or unfamiliar the situations were for me, I kept trying to think of how the women must feel. How terrified they must feel to be in a situation so completely out of their control. And that further prompted me to learn more about the different mental health conditions, hoping with more knowledge I could provide better care. I quickly learnt, mental health couldn't be learnt fully from a textbook.

As this was happening at work, mental health issues started to become prominent in my home life too. No matter how much knowledge I have from a healthcare provider's perspective, nothing compares to the personal experience of caring for a loved one.

Friends, family, and people I care deeply about began suffering from a wide array of mental health conditions. I had to learn about

Borderline Personality Disorder, Emotionally Unstable Personality Disorder, Bipolar Disorder, Complex PTSD, Social Anxiety, Chronic Depression, and Harm OCD, just to name a few.

I learnt how to help the people I love identify triggers for their anxious or depressive episodes, and what I can do to help. I went with them to more appointments than I can count, and asked all the questions I could, in an effort to understand. I went with them to counselling sessions, and supported them through CBT and other forms of therapy. I helped them to help themselves.

Learning how to help and support them was hard, and such an individualised process. But mostly I learnt that sometimes the best support I can give is to leave them alone, to give them the space they need, and allow them to be alone in their own head, which is often the loneliest, scariest place to be.

Even though I sat in all their sessions, and listened to all the ways their conditions affected them, I still couldn't fully relate. Don't get me wrong, we've all had our bad days. We've all allowed something to get us down to the point we struggle to see a way out. This is simply an extreme response to normal emotions.

I thought, after everything that had happened in both my personal and professional life, I'd experienced all aspects of mental health care. That I understood the challenges people face, and how they can overcome them. I thought that no matter what life threw at me and my loved ones, I would know how to fight it. I had all the knowledge, the experience, and the tools that I needed. I had it all—or so I thought.

Ten years ago, my life changed irrevocably. In the blink of an eye, I lost the whole future I had seen for myself. I dreamt of getting married, having children, getting promoted to my ideal job, and living the dream that I always thought I wanted.

You see, ten years ago I was diagnosed with a chronic, life-changing, degenerative condition that is effectively a terminal diagnosis. The condition I have is called Multiple Sclerosis, or MS for short. It's an auto-immune condition where essentially my own body attacks itself. The slightest hint of an infection, stress, lack of sleep, etc, and my immune system goes into overdrive and gets confused. It can't differentiate between normal brain matter and illness.

Without getting too technical, that confusion is what causes scarring on my brain or spinal cord. Wherever the scar is located, that influences what symptoms I will experience.

It could be I get a scar that causes me to lose feeling in one arm, or another that takes away the sight in one of my eyes. It can be as minor as some pins and needles in my hands or feet, or be extreme, causing me to lose the use of my legs. It literally is pot luck, depending on which symptom you get, how long you experience the symptoms for, and how quickly they improve. Most will get better, but they won't ever return to how they were before. Like with any scar, though it may fade, it will always be there. I think that's one of the hardest things to get my head around. The unknown. The lack of control.

With the type of MS that I have, known as relapse remitting, it means I have periods where the MS symptoms flare up—that's the relapse part—and then times when I'm in recovery—the remitting part.

Before I was diagnosed, I'd experienced symptoms that I now know are MS, but at the time, I blamed them on lots of other things. I was exhausted all the time, like my body physically felt too heavy to the point I wanted to sleep constantly. But at the time, I was working thirteen-hour shifts as a midwife, often two or three in a row, including night shifts, and so it was easy to blame my fatigue on that.

I thought I just needed more sleep, since my sleep had started to suffer. A combination of exhaustion and increasing pain meant I was waking up frequently overnight and struggling to get back to sleep. It felt like a vicious cycle because the more my symptoms affected me, the less sleep I got. Then the reduced sleep led to more problems.

However, it wasn't until I had some life changing symptoms that I sought medical help. I lost all the sight in my right eye, which I have to admit is one of the most terrifying experiences I've ever been through. I can't even begin to describe the fear I felt wondering when or if my vision would ever return, and if it did, would it be back to normal.

While I was seeking help for my reduced vision, the relapse hit harder, taking away the feeling in my right leg. I couldn't weight-bare, or feel it at all. It was like I had an alien limb. I could see it, but I couldn't use it. I felt so broken. At this stage, I didn't know what the problem was, and I was terrified wondering what the hell could cause these types of symptoms.

Of course, my brain ran rampant, wondering if it was something really serious—brain tumour, cancer, or so much more. But, despite having medical training, I never saw MS coming.

I still remember the appointment when I was given my diagnosis. The doctor told me the MRI and lumbar puncture both showed I have MS. After that, she basically gave me an info leaflet and said the MS nurse would be in touch to discuss what happens next.

I walked out of that appointment, and my life was changed forever. I mean, realistically, I was no sicker, and nothing physically had changed during that ten-minute appointment. So why did I feel like my world had ended?

I guess the only new thing was this label I had been given. Nobody could see this label, and in reality, nobody would know about it unless I told them. But I knew I was now officially labelled as *disabled*.

I was twenty-four years old, and I felt like I'd just been handed a death sentence, and sent home to deal with it. I can't even begin to explain how overwhelmed I felt with it all. Not only was I dealing with the physical issues that I now know to be a relapse, but I also had to come to terms with the idea that this isn't an illness that can be cured with some pills. This is something that has no cure, and will one day end my life. The weight of that knowledge, at such a young age, consumed me.

I had just started seeing an amazing guy. We went on our first date in March 2013, and I think I knew from that first date that we had potential. I'd been on more than my share of disastrous dates, and kissed my fair share of frogs, so I knew a good guy when I saw him. He didn't want anything serious, and at the start, I was fine with that.

In June, just four months after our first date, I had the relapse that led to my diagnosis. Despite us not really being in a relationship, he stepped up whilst I was sick. He visited me in hospital, he met my family—even though we said we weren't doing things like that—and he generally cared for me, despite me telling him he didn't have to.

Every night I was in hospital, he would Facetime me to say goodnight, and we would talk about all the funny things I had seen that day on the ward—he loved trying to make me laugh and forget about where I was. I tried to tell myself it was just because we were friends, nothing more. I think we both knew our relationship was heading somewhere, even if we weren't brave enough to voice it. But all that changed when I got diagnosed.

I felt like I would ultimately become a burden to everyone around me, as all I could think about was the worst-case scenario. I didn't want him to end up being my carer. The thing I feared more than anything was the idea that he would stay with me out of some misguided loyalty, rather than because he genuinely wanted to. I didn't want anybody's pity.

Reacting to my own insecurities, I told him I didn't want to see him again. I pushed him away because I was afraid. Dating a person who is labelled as disabled comes with a lot of issues—or, at least, in my depressed mind, it did. Thankfully, he didn't allow me to push him away. He wanted to keep spending time with me, getting to know me, and he promised that he would never let his decision to stay or go be determined by my condition. I wasn't sure I believed him, but I didn't have much choice in the matter, as he held on tight, no matter how hard I pushed.

Looking back, I think the depression probably crept up on me slowly, but at the time it didn't feel that way. It felt like I was hit by a brick wall, and I couldn't get over it. It was more than just feeling down, my whole world felt pointless. The darkness seemed to invade every little part of my body, and I didn't even know how to function. Some days, just getting out of bed felt like completing a marathon.

Initially, I thought the best way to get over how I was feeling was to just tell myself I was fine. I told myself that since I was never going to get better, I needed to just get on with my life. So as soon as I could use my leg enough, and my vision had recovered, I went straight back to work. I pretended I didn't have a limp, and that I was just tired.

When people asked me if I was okay, I flippantly told them I had been diagnosed with MS. Some of my work colleagues were concerned I didn't fully appreciate the gravity of the diagnosis. They were right. My head just wasn't in the right place, and burying my head in the sand seemed to be the only option.

I was thinking, if I pretend it's not real, maybe it won't be. In reality, all the stress, exhaustion, and lack of sleep that I was ignoring were the ideal scenario to produce another relapse, which is what happened. This time, it was just a milder version of the last relapse, but I hated the fact my eyesight deteriorated again, and I was back to limping, unable to feel my leg properly.

It was around this time I finally got an appointment to see the MS nurse at the hospital. Of course, as soon as I saw her, I repeated the mantra I was living by, telling her I was fine. I still remember the way she looked at me. She had the typical 'stern nurse stare' down to perfection. She called me out on my bullshit, and told me that I was lying to myself. That nobody comes to terms with a diagnosis like this so quickly, and I knew she was right. I don't know if I was doing it because I didn't want to deal with it, or because I didn't know how.

The nurse was amazing, and she told me that the first thing I needed to do, to help me get on top of the relapses, is to start Disease Modifying Therapy. Although there is no cure for MS, there are medications that help in different ways. The aim of them is to reduce the frequency of the relapses, and to reduce the severity of them when they do happen.

To me, this was a bright light in the darkness that was casting shadows over my life. But the nurse said she wasn't prepared to recommend therapy for me until I truly accepted my diagnosis. The thing was, I had no idea how to do that. I felt like she was giving me this ray of hope, but making me jump through hoops before I could get there.

I went home with more bloody leaflets, and a whole lot more doom. That's how I started to feel, like my world was just filled with an impending feeling of doom, and slowly I started to retreat from everyone and everything.

I allowed the darkness to consume me, and I pulled away from everyone. I began calling in sick for work, as I genuinely couldn't even get out of bed, let alone try and care for other people.

The only real human company I had was when the guy I was seeing came over every weekend. We hung out in my flat, and he generally just tried to distract me. I never told him that was the last thing I should be doing. I liked the distraction. I liked those days when I could just hang out with him and feel normal all over again. But then came the day he had to go back home for work, and I had to go back to reality.

Those days hit me hard. If you imagine the time I had with him, escaping from reality, those days were my drug. I chased the high of those days, and the normality that came with them. So when I had to be without my drug, it felt like I was withdrawing, going cold turkey. The darkness overtook me with a vengeance.

As I mentioned, my MS relapses take effect overnight. I wake up in the morning with a new set of symptoms, and quite honestly, it's terrifying having no control over that.

When the doctor and nurse gave me all the leaflets, to help me become more prepared, I don't think they had any idea how much crippling anxiety it would cause me. Sometimes being forewarned is forearmed, but for me, knowledge actually made me worse.

You see, MS has several varying stages, but the most publicly talked about are the severe forms of MS. The ones that leave you bedbound, needing a wheelchair, incontinent, or completely dependent on the care of other people. For me, it was like I was looking into a future that scared the shit out of me. None of that fit into the perfect future I had laid out for myself.

The fear started to consume me, and I was absolutely terrified of waking up in the morning, wondering how the hell MS would affect me that day. Every time I opened my eyes, I did a mental check to ensure everything was in full working order, but this only added to my stress levels.

It got to the point where I literally couldn't fall asleep. I told myself that if I stayed awake, I couldn't wake up with new symptoms. I know the logical part of my mind knew it didn't work like that, but I was no longer being guided by my logical brain.

Naturally, my poor life choices were a breeding ground for poor health, and I had another relapse—this time losing the feeling in my left arm. My MS nurse said there's no time for me to come to terms with things on my own anymore, since I clearly had no intention of doing that anyway. She basically informed me that if I didn't start MS treatment, the future I was so terrified of would get one step closer. So she arranged for me to see a therapist.

By the time my first appointment came around, my depression had a hold of me. I didn't look forward to anything, nor did I really leave the house. The only thing that I could rely on during that time was the escape I got from diving into a good book. But again, I was using that as a way of escaping my reality, as opposed to dealing with life.

To say I didn't have high hopes for my therapy session was an understatement. I just didn't think one session talking to someone would help overcome the all-consuming anxiety and depression that had a hold on me.

Sadly, I was right.

The appointment barely scratched the surface of my issues, and I think it made the hospital more aware of how deep within my depression I truly was. The reality was, I'd reached the stage where I didn't want help. I didn't want to get better, because I would never truly be healthy.

In my distorted mind, all I could think was that I would just be getting my mind better, only for my body to deteriorate further, which was my worst nightmare. I didn't want to become the vision of a disabled person with MS that I had in my head. And the appointment made me realise why I didn't want help. It boils down to the fact, I no longer wanted to live.

I ignored those feelings for as long as I could, and most of the time I could push them away. I could distract myself with a good book, or hanging out with the guy, who was still doing a great job at distracting me. But the feelings always hovered over me, and when the darkness got too much, it was easier for those harmful thoughts to sneak in.

I hit rock bottom, and it scared me enough to call my mum. I cried down the phone and told her everything. She helped me arrange a doctor's appointment with the same man I'd seen for years, and is still my GP now. I felt pure shame as I confessed how bad my life had really got, and I talked about how scared I was of the future. He was the first person who told me that whilst there is a dark and scary, extreme side to MS, that's not what the majority experiences. Most people get it under control and manage to live good lives.

I told him I didn't believe him, that I had read that MS was a terminal diagnosis, which technically it is. Thanks to advances in medicine—which are still happening—MS only takes around ten years off your life expectancy. But actually, the number one cause of death amongst people with MS is suicide. That's still a statistic, even today.

I was so close to becoming yet another depressing statistic.

My GP felt I needed more psychological help than I had been offered, and he set me up with a local mental health charity who provides counselling to people who need it quicker than they can get it on the NHS.

I arranged my first session, and my family made sure I attended. I had very little hope, and honestly, I still wasn't sure if I even wanted help. I couldn't see much point in living my life this way, and those thoughts were getting stronger as time went on.

Whether I liked it or not, my life changed the day I was diagnosed, and that was something I had to come to terms with. Since then, it's continued to change irrevocably, and my therapist made it clear to me that if I didn't find a way to learn to cope now, I wouldn't have a future. She told me I had to grieve for the loss of the future I saw for myself, as that had been stolen from me. She said it's okay to grieve something you've lost, as it's the only way to prepare you for the life that's left behind.

This is when she introduced a new concept to me, and I remember at the time I thought she was the one who had lost the plot, and not me. She told me I had to make friends with my monster.

MS was a monster that had invaded my life, and it was holding me hostage, but now was the time to take back my life. But I knew that the monster wasn't going anywhere. I could continue ignoring it, or trying to fight it, but the fact remains, it will always be there. So she suggested something I had never even considered. Not just accept it, but make friends with it.

Her advice was for me to go home and tell my MS exactly how I was feeling. Tell it all the ways it had a grip on my life, and all the ways I wanted it to fuck off. I remember looking at her like she was crazy, but I had nothing to lose.

I went home, and in the middle of the night, when all my body wanted to do was sleep, but my brain wouldn't allow it, I decided to do as I was told. I can tell you right now, it's probably the weirdest thing I've ever done, but it's also one of the most cathartic.

I pictured this monster sitting in a chair at the bottom of my bed. I conjured him up in my mind to the point that if someone had asked me to draw him, I would have been able to—if I could actually draw. That's how much detail I went into.

At first I felt strange, but then I just opened myself up to it, and I embraced the idea. I talked, opening up about the life I wanted and the life I thought I'd lost. Whilst the process didn't obviously get me any answers, what it did do is teach me that I can open up. After that, I put my trust in my counsellor, and I talked to her about all the things that were causing me to feel overwhelmed.

It wasn't an overnight success, and it took me nine months to fully get myself back into a good position. Even now, when I have a relapse that I struggle to cope with, I go back to the teachings that I learnt, and I talk it through with my monster. The more I talked it through, the more the mist seemed to clear. The depression and anxiety that had a hold of me seemed to lessen, and I was able to think clearer. Though it's still the case that every time I have a bad day, where I'm feeling ill or exhausted, they find a way to creep back up to the surface.

I've come to accept that just like the MS monster, the anxiety and depression are like little pets that come alongside it. They will always be there, just under the surface, waiting for the right time to try and take back control for themselves. But just like with MS, I fight every day to keep control, and to keep them hidden.

My life did change ten years ago, but not necessarily for the worst. I had a career as a midwife planned out, but the health complications that came with MS meant I couldn't work in such a high-pressure job. When I had to give up my career, I was lost. I didn't think I could do anything else, it's all I'd done since school. But, when I was grieving the loss of midwifery, I found a way to distract myself from the depression. I started writing books, and that led me to where I am now. Actually, to say that is a massive understatement. Now I get to do something I adore, living a life I never saw coming, and I love every single minute of it. Who knew listening to the voices in my head could be an actual career? One I'm good at, and that has opened up so many amazing doors for me. I've done signings both in the UK and US, and it humbles me every time someone asks for my signature or a picture with me. This life gave me a reason to strive for more, and I will forever be grateful for that.

The other part of my life I stressed about was finding love. I worried that nobody could love me with MS. Well... it just so happens, the guy I met just five months before I was diagnosed, he did stick around, and has done for the last ten years.

Mr Luna became my rock, and he's the reason I keep going each and every day. Without the love and support he shows me, not just with my health, but also my book career, I would be lost. He doesn't see me as a disabled person he has to care for, I'm his partner, and we look after each other, just like any good couple does. I am the person I am today because he's by my side.

He makes me laugh when I want to cry, and he holds me when I'm scared. Each time my monster and its pets threaten to take hold of me, he helps me to fight them off. He's the love of my life, and even if he never wants to marry me—though I really hope he will—he still makes me the happiest person in the world. He's my soulmate.

I was diagnosed with MS ten years ago, and I wouldn't say I'm exactly friends with my monster (and its pets), but we live harmoniously in one body. Mental health issues are still prominent in my life, and the darkness still takes over sometimes. When this happens, I just have to go back to what I learnt, making sure to always talk it through with someone and not bottle it up.

Thanks to the techniques I learnt, my relationships have improved. I communicate more with my mum, who is my best friend, and she helps me every day. The people in my life know me better, all because I learnt to befriend a side of myself I didn't want to accept. I can't stress it enough when I say that you don't have to do it alone, no matter what you're going through. It's okay to ask for help.

I thought I couldn't ask for help, as I should know what to do, I should know how to help myself. I let the fear build up, and it consumed me. Whereas if I'd spoken to someone and not let the worst-case scenario grow in my mind, I wouldn't have needed to hit rock bottom. So never be afraid to ask for help, as it may just save your life. I know it did mine.

My dad gave me the best piece of advice that I still live by. "Enjoy the good days and live them to the fullest, because those memories are what will help you fight off your demons and get you through the bad days."

WRITING IS MY SUPERPOWER

by T.F. Webb

I LIVE MY LIFE BY numbers, even though I love words.

Three is the number of times I check the door before I go to bed at night. Five is the number of times I do complete each movement I use to wash my hands. One is the number I press my thumb to the keyhole so that it can leave an imprint, so that I don't have to check the door, again, and again, and again. And the lists I make go on, and on, and on...

Yet my story is much like others, even if it's my own. How did I stray so far from the words, into the numbers, only to find my way home?

It began with an eight. At eight years old (there or thereabouts) when I wrote my first story, complete with illustrations, and won second place in a local poetry competition. I had been reading for many years, and was doing well. But sometimes a vivid imagination needs a life of its own, so I let mine roam. And roam it did – onto paper, with pen or paint, or just feasting on the words. It was heaven. But (as with all good things) this stage of my life wouldn't last.

At around 12 years old, my family and I moved away from everything we knew and held dear. The suburban landscape was so very different from the countryside we'd lived in. People were more competitive, more confident; just more. My introverted nature meant it was harder to fit in, but when I did finally make friends, I lost the most vital part of me. I still read compulsively, but I did not write again.

The first sign that something wasn't quite right was at age 15. That is when the door checking began. I would leave the house, get to the end of the street then have to walk all the way back to check the door to make sure it was locked. It took me a while to figure out that if I pressed my thumb to the keyhole, I could check for the imprint at the end of the road and know it was all okay. It seems excessive, right? But if I didn't do this, that thought would invade my mind, stake its claim, and remain there until I went back and checked the damned door. Otherwise I'd feel panicked, shaky, and short of breath.

Of course, there were several moments of trauma that happened during my teenage years that helped to poke and prod at this excessive door checking, one of which was a relationship where I was subjected to emotional and physical abuse. This is where my opinions on domestic violence were formed, especially towards those instances that occur in teenage relationships. I appreciate there are people that have been through much more than me, I've met them. However, the experience affected me through my later teenage years and still affects me now.

At around 25 years old I moved back to the West Country, and within a short space of time I found myself drawn towards Higher Education. As a mature student without A levels, I had to complete an Access to Higher Education certificate. This experience would re-ignite my passion for reading and formed the basis for me beginning to write again. I thrived in an environment where I could immerse myself in books. Whether it was poetry, prose, or plays, I revelled in the words. But, whilst I couldn't be happier surrounded by books and was lucky to have an incredible English Tutor (I have been blessed in that department throughout my life), I was still anxious. I was still door-checking. I was also now listing everything. To-do lists became a staple in my life. And counting? That became central to it.

The problem was (and still is) that I would count the number of times I tried the door handle at night to check it was locked, and I would count how many times I performed specific movements every time I washed my hands. I would count out the most insignificant things, although they never were to me. Although I received my certificate, this condition would begin to impact the way I learned. It became my nemesis. I ended up dropping out of university, as the stress was too great and the symptoms too much to handle.

In 2004, one of the greatest moments of my life happened. I had my first child, my son. He was the mellowest, most chilled out baby I had ever met. I should have been so totally lost in him, such was the love that I had for him. Instead, I found myself lost in a cycle of hand washing, terrified by the idea of contaminating him with any germs I may have picked up. Every time I picked him up, I would wash my hands, and count the movements time after time, after time. This is the first time I decided to seek help.

When my son was around six months old, I contacted my GP. I explained to them what was happening, and how it was impacting my ability to be a mother. I was put onto a wonderful lady, who told me what I was experiencing was called OCD (Obsessive Compulsive Disorder). She explained that it was more than likely due to the incidents that had occurred all those years ago, and whilst my obsessive thoughts could be irrational, they were not stupid (as I continuously labelled them). She suggested journaling to help with trying to rationalise why I was having the thoughts, whether I was having a good or bad day, and making note of the compulsions so that I could try to limit them when they began to surface. And that was that. I wasn't given medication then, and I haven't been prescribed it now. I just adopted the process of scrawling down the ramblings in my head, and carried on.

After the birth of my daughter, I returned to university, this time to study English Literature. One of the modules that we covered during the first year was Creative Writing. It was this that saved me. The more time I spent writing, the more the thoughts that invaded my mind were pushed to one side. It turned out that immersing myself in other worlds distracted me from the obsessive thoughts that frequently addled my brain. Getting the characters and their stories onto the paper from the film reel in my mind gave me great comfort and joy. I was limited for time with two children under five and other modules to complete, but I began to make endless notes, and also collecting ways in which to prompt ideas in my head. Newspapers were my greatest resource at that point in time. So I made an effort to buy local and national papers a couple of times a week.

Of course all good things come to an end. But whilst graduation came and went, my need to write did not waiver. In the early 2010s, I met someone who shared my love of words. Someone who loved to write and read like me. We would discuss our writing over coffee, and began to bounce ideas off each other. It was at this point that I decided to develop one of my short stories that I had written at university into a novel (one that, sadly, remains incomplete to this day). The encouragement and support that I received from my friend and some family members drove me forward. I began to write more, try different forms of writing (such as poetry), and learn more about writing through taking short courses to learn about the genres.

By 2014, I had submitted my first short story for publication. Whilst having to have two people (a different friend and a family member) stand over me to make me press the send button on the email, I don't regret it. It was published, and this made me happy. Until I wasn't.

During this time my OCD was a footnote in my life, and my anxiety was low. I was still listing, and hand washing, but these compulsions weren't taking over my life as my obsessive thoughts were at a minimum. My need to write was my new obsession. It turned out that focusing on writing was the best way to alleviate the thoughts that lead to the compulsions, a fact that was a great relief. But, it only takes one thing to undo a good thing, and unfortunately it was me that was my own undoing.

As part of being a writer, it is important to be present on social media. It is a great place to chat with like-minded people, and also to find things to help prompt me when I suffered with writer's block. Unfortunately (more than likely due to my OCD) I became too involved, and it took me away from writing, which was the very reason I was there in the first place. I found myself hopelessly addicted to being online, and justified my lack of writing by convincing myself that if I was adding things to my social media such as general musings and occasional poetry, it was still writing, wasn't it?

It was, of course. What it wasn't though was the novel I was supposed to be writing. As freeing as it was to write online, it became a burden when I was finding myself logging in multiple times a day. It was a messy situation that lasted far too long, and in the end the only way I could deal with it was to go cold turkey. It was hard, and I will be eternally grateful to the people who advised me to leave. In the long term it was worth it, because as soon as it was under control, I was able to write again. That is how I was able to complete the book with my writing partner. That is how I managed to begin to find myself again. That is where I found my peace.

My thoughts still fluctuate depending on my anxiety levels, although sometimes it would appear as though they work independently of any anxiousness I may be feeling. Following the pandemic, I decided it was time to finally get some help. I wanted to make sure that my ability to function for my family was not further impaired due to stressful events that have unfolded over the past few years. I also wanted to make sure that I had ways to cope apart from writing, especially as I do have those times when writer's block can hit me unexpectedly. During the session, my anxiety was confirmed through the GAD7 and my OCD score came in higher than expected. The recommendation made was that I would need high intensity CBT (Cognitive Behavioural Therapy), followed by one-to-one sessions. Unfortunately, there are no therapists available at this time for the CBT component of my treatment, and I cannot attend the one-to-one sessions until this is completed. So in the meantime, I have been offered a CBT course online until there is someone available to help me. I'm glad I took this step. It means I will be able to move forward in real life. But what of writing?

Writing has been, and will always be my balm. It soothes my anxiety, and expels those intrusive thoughts. It helps me escape the world, and inject some much-needed comedy, drama, and colour into my life. Whilst the treatment I get will give me other coping mechanisms, and a way to deal with the traumas of my past, it will purely be a supplement to the undoubted catharsis writing has provided me with. I write because I love to. I write because it heals me a little more every day.

Writing is my superpower, because it takes the pain away.

Thanks

THANK YOU FOR READING, AND of course, thank you to all the authors who wrote something—especially a friend of mine Paula, who is not an author, but who bravely agreed when I asked her to write me something about T1—being that it was something I knew very little about, really. Long-term physical illness, like T1, can impact mental health detrimentally. But we don't talk about it nearly enough. We see labels here, there and everywhere, but never, truly, what goes on beneath.

I think we can all agree this collection as a whole is rather staggering in its breadth, depth and complexity. Here, real people talk about real, and sometimes very, very scary conditions they or a loved one had no control over. No, we don't cover everything, but we do cover an awful, awful lot of things that are REALLY, REALLY HARD to talk about.

If you meet any of these authors in person (the ones who've been able to add their names to their articles, anyway), please congratulate them on their sheer and utter bravery.

There are some pieces by "anonymous" and the reasons for this are various, but if you figure it out who wrote the anonymous ones, please respect that author and keep it to yourself.

These words are extremely private; souls, hearts and minds laid totally bare.

I had no idea what I'd receive in my inbox, when I came up with this idea at surely a ridiculous time of night when all my "good" ideas hit. So to say I've been humbled, surprised, shocked, saddened, enlightened and comforted is an understatement.

For me, this little book just proves—as I said in the beginning—you are never alone.

Never

SML x x

More Information

Anything we make from the sale of this book is being shared equally between the Samaritans and the mental health chat service, Shout.

Find out more giveusashout.org and samaritans.org

We're selling physical copies at our signing event Authors at the Armouries where all of our authors will be in attendance.

You can find out more info about how to get hold of a signed copy by visiting our FB Group or Instagram Page

www.facebook.com/groups/smlevents
www.instagram.com/authorsatthearmouries

Printed in Great Britain
by Amazon